Anti Inflammatory Diet Cookbook

How to Reduce Inflammation with Top Anti-Inflammatory Foods. Over 100 Easy, Healthy, and Tasty Recipes That Will Make You Feel Better Than Ever & Restore Overall Health

Dorothy Smith

© Copyright 2019 by Dorothy Smith - All rights reserved.

This content is provided with the sole purpose of providing relevant information on a specific topic for which every reasonable effort has been made to ensure that it is both accurate and reasonable. Nevertheless, by purchasing this content, you consent to the fact that the author, as well as the publisher, are in no way experts on the topics contained herein, regardless of any claims as such that may be made within. As such, any suggestions or recommendations that are made within are done so purely for entertainment value. It is recommended that you always consult a professional prior to undertaking any of the advice or techniques discussed within.

This is a legally binding declaration that is considered both valid and fair by both the Committee of Publishers Association and the American Bar Association and should be considered as legally binding within the United States.

The reproduction, transmission, and duplication of any of the content found herein, including any specific or extended information, will be done as an illegal act regardless of the end form the information ultimately takes. This includes copied versions of the work, both physical, digital, and audio, unless express consent of the Publisher is provided beforehand. Any additional rights reserved.

Furthermore, the information that can be found within the pages described forthwith shall be considered both accurate and truthful when it comes to the recounting of facts. As such, any use, correct or incorrect, of the provided information will render the Publisher free of responsibility as to the actions taken outside of their direct purview. Regardless, there are zero scenarios where the original author or the Publisher can be deemed liable in any fashion for any damages or hardships that may result from any of the information discussed herein.

Additionally, the information in the following pages is intended only for informational purposes and should thus be thought of as universal. As befitting its nature, it is presented without assurance regarding its prolonged validity or interim quality. Trademarks that are mentioned are done without written consent and can in no way be considered an endorsement from the trademark holder.

Table of Contents

Chapter 1: Introduction to Anti-Inflammatory Foods . 1
    What is the Anti-Inflammatory Diet? 1
    Top Anti-Inflammatory Foods 2
        Tomatoes 2
        Olive Oil 2
        Olives 3
        Dark Leafy Green Vegetables 3
        Berries and Citrus Fruits 4
        Nuts and seeds 4
        Fish 5
        Coffee 6
    Foods to Avoid: Inflammatory Foods 6
        Refined Foods 6
        Soda and Sugary Beverages 7
        Red Meat 7
        Deep-Fried Foods 8
        Processed Meats 9
        Pasta, White Bread, and Gluten 9
        High-Fructose Corn Syrup 10

Chapter 2: The Benefits of Following an Anti-Inflammatory Diet 14
    Health and Lifestyle Benefits of Anti-Inflammatory Foods 14
    How do Anti-Inflammatory Foods Work? 14
    Focus on Healthy Nuts and Seeds 15

Chapter 3: Smoothies and Beverages 25

Smoothies (Dairy and Plant-based).....................25
- Avocado and Coconut Milk Smoothie 26
- Mangos, Bananas, and Peaches Smoothie 29
- Freshly Brewed Coffee 33
- Hot Chocolate...36
- Freshly Squeezed Juices...............................39

Chapter 4: Soups and Stews 42

Light Soups and Broths..................................42
- Bone Broth 42
- Consommé Soups 48
- Lean Beef Chili 50

Chapter 5: Sides, Snacks, and Salads 57

Fresh, Homemade Salads..................................57

Types of Kale, Spinach, and Arugula 58
- Types of Kale 58
- Types of Spinach 60
- Types of Arugula 61
- Kale and Tahini Salad 67
- Spinach and Cranberry Salad 69

Snacks and Sides for Any Time of the Day (and On the Go) 71
- Kale Chips 72

Chapter 6: Plant-based Anti-Inflammatory Foods 84

Eating Vegan and Anti-inflammatory: The Benefits of Combining Both..84

Plant-based Recipes and Food Ideas 85
- Tempeh Skillet Plate..................................89
- Guacamole 90

Lentil Daal 93

Chapter 7: Meats, Poultry, and Seafood 101

Seafood Recipes 101

Baked Salmon in Garlic Sauce 101

Tuna and Avocado Tacos 102

Oven Roast Chicken 107

Chapter 8: Desserts 116

Cakes and Pie Recipes 116

Chocolate Cake 116

Pumpkin Cake 118

Rhubarb and Strawberry Pie 120

Puddings, Custards, and Ice Cream Desserts 124

Peanut Butter and Banana Ice Cream 131

Chapter 9: Conclusion and FAQ's 134

Tips and Suggestions 134

Frequently Asked Questions 138

Chapter 1: Introduction to Anti-Inflammatory Foods

What is the Anti-Inflammatory Diet?

The anti-inflammatory diet is a practical, healthy way of eating that treats and prevents inflammation associated with many chronic conditions and illnesses. Inflammation occurs in the body to fight disease or infection, though it can happen when there is the presence of autoimmune conditions that can trigger unnecessary flare-ups, causing pain and discomfort. When inflammation becomes a regular occurrence itself as a faulty action (as a result of a health condition, but not to heal the body), it can be a serious hindrance in feeling and functioning well. Preventing inflammation can be done successfully through diet, and this includes significant relief from many conditions, including arthritis, psoriasis, colitis, inflammatory bowel disease, and respiratory conditions (asthma, bronchitis). Due to the nutrient-richness of this diet, there are further benefits including significant weight loss and the successful treatment of diabetes (regulating insulin levels), heart disease, lupus, and heart disease.

Metabolism and an overall sense of feeling well are further advantages of the anti-inflammatory diet.

Top Anti-Inflammatory Foods

One of the most effective methods in treating inflammation is diet. Building a diet that is rich in nutrients and ingredients that halt or prevent inflammation is key to a more productive, healthy lifestyle. There are some key foods and nutrients to include in your everyday meal plans:

Tomatoes

A versatile fruit, and often considered a vegetable, tomatoes are an excellent source of vitamins and fiber. They can be added to a wide variety of meals, including pasta, salads, and sandwiches, or simply enjoyed on their own. Easily enjoyed raw, stewed, or pureed into a sauce, adding tomatoes to your diet, if you haven't already, is both a healthy and tasty way to improve your diet.

Olive Oil

Containing healthy fats, olive oil is an excellent choice for many dishes, including sauces, marinades, and for use in cooking. Using olive oil in everyday cooking is a great option, and it's relatively easy and inexpensive to buy extra virgin olive oil, which is available in most grocery stores. Always choose the dark bottle, which helps the oil preserve its freshness. Olive oil is high in monounsaturated fats, which are the healthiest variety. It protects against heart disease, prevents strokes, and improves cognitive function, in addition to having anti-inflammatory properties.

Olives

Olives are tasty and an excellent source of vitamin E, as well as many other antioxidants. They make a great addition to salads, sandwiches, or as a snack with low-fat cheese or vegetables. Olives contain a lot of healthy fats and are a staple in Mediterranean dishes, which is one of the top reasons why Mediterranean cuisine is considered one of the healthiest in the world. Adding just a small portion of olives to your diet can make a significant impact on your health.

Dark Leafy Green Vegetables

Spinach, arugula, and kale are top-notch foods in the anti-inflammatory food group and have a significant impact on many other body functions. They contain vitamins K and C, iron, magnesium, and calcium. Dark greens also contain a lot of antioxidants, which is key to giving them anti-inflammatory powers. Adding any one or all of these leafy foods to your diet is a sure way to improving your diet and health.

Berries and Citrus Fruits

Rich in antioxidants, fiber, and delicious, fruits are an excellent choice for reducing inflammation associated with disease and chronic conditions. While they are seasonal and their availability can vary, certain fruits can be purchased frozen or fresh. They are high in vitamin C and often cited for preventing colds and improving immunity function. Berries are versatile in that they are easy to eat as a snack on their own, though can be added to a variety of recipes, including smoothies, desserts, puddings, and salads.

Nuts and seeds

Almonds, hazelnuts, cashews, pecans, walnuts, and pistachios are among some of the many delicious and nutrient-heavy nuts that can be easily added or supplemented to your diet. If you are vegan, you'll want to include as many nuts and seeds in your diet as possible to get the most out of the nutrients they contain such as protein, fiber, omega 6 and 3 fats, and many vitamins and minerals, including iron, magnesium, and vitamin E. Just a small dose each day can make a significant difference in your health. Nuts and seeds, including chia seeds, pumpkin, sesame, and sunflower seeds, also contain a high number of vitamins and minerals, making them an ideal topping or ingredient in salads, desserts, baked goods, or as a snack on their own.

Fish

Fatty fish, such as salmon, is an excellent source of protein, calcium, and healthy fats. To reduce inflammation, focus on eating salmon and tuna, as both are high in protein, calcium, and healthy fats and contain no sugars or carbohydrates, which contribute to a lot of health conditions. If you are accustomed to eating red meat frequently, slowly replacing some of your beef or pork dishes with salmon or tuna is a great idea, as it reduces the number of inflammatory foods and gives you a good reason to try new recipes! When shopping for fish, always aim for fresh or frozen fish. If you choose canned salmon or tuna, choose fresh catch and fish in general that are naturally sourced, so that it is a higher quality.

Other fish to consider trying and adding to your diet include mackerel, sardines, and white fish, which are also high in protein, calcium and healthy fats.

Coffee

As much as some studies and opinions target coffee as unhealthy, it has benefits that we may not realize until we read about them. Many people avoid coffee because of the effects of caffeine, though in moderate portions, it can reap many benefits. These are discussed further in the drinks and beverages section of the book, which includes some options for enjoying coffee and other hot drinks.

Foods to Avoid: Inflammatory Foods

Refined Foods

In general, all foods that are processed and high in carbohydrates should be avoided or limited as much as possible. If you find yourself craving a box of cookies or a bag of potato chips, skip the snack aisle completely. Instead, look for dried fruits, nuts, and seeds as a healthier way to fulfill your craving. Processed foods offer little to no nutritional benefits, and often contain a lot of artificial additives and hidden sugars.

Soda and Sugary Beverages

Sweetened iced teas, soda, and juices should be avoided. Sugary beverages can become addictive and difficult to replace with water or tea, which are better options, though there are some alternatives to consider, such as unsweetened iced teas, low carb sweetened sodas and sparkling water with natural fruit flavoring. Avoid diet sodas, which contain harmful artificial sweeteners, and instead, search for drinks that contain stevia (a low carb sweetener) or natural options, such as honey or syrup.

Red Meat

In moderation, small portions of red meat can contribute to a healthy diet. It's important to minimize or reduce the portion and alternate with other protein options such as poultry, fish, and tofu (as well as other vegan substitutes). On the other hand, consuming large portions of beef, pork, etc. can lead to heart disease and high blood pressure, especially if you don't eat enough plant-based foods. Balance is key, and while eliminating red meat completely is ideal, it can also be significantly reduced with good results.

Deep-Fried Foods

French fries, fried meats, and even deep-fried vegetables should avoid as much as possible. The taste and texture may be tempting, though these foods contain trans fats or "unhealthy" fats that contribute to many diseases, such as cancer, heart conditions, and asthma. If they become a regular part of your diet, they can increase the production of free radicals in the body, which increases the likelihood of cancerous growth and other conditions. Craving fast foods and convenience snacks, such as cookies or chips, can be addictive over time, making an effort to switch to a healthier alternative challenging.

If you find ditching fast food difficult, consider healthier options on the menu, such as salads, baked potatoes, and soups. If you have the choice between deep-fried or baked, baked food may seem less appealing at first, though it can be delicious once you become accustomed to it.

Processed Meats

All processed meats should be avoided. This includes pre-packaged sliced deli meats, smoked meats, and anything that contains nitrates and carcinogens, both of which contribute to inflammation and some forms of cancer. Smoked meats can be enjoyed on occasion, though should be left off the menu as much as possible. For example, if you enjoy smoked salmon with capers as a treat now and again, this is acceptable. However, eating smoked hams, sausage, and other meats on a daily or even weekly basis should be avoided.

Pasta, White Bread, and Gluten

While not everyone may agree with ditching pasta, bread, and gluten entirely unless there is a condition that requires complete avoidance of gluten. Most foods in this category lack nutrition and are basically considered "filler" foods, which are often used as a supplement with meats and vegetables. White bread, for example, is void of nutrients, which makes whole-grain options a better choice overall. Pasta doesn't have to be skipped if you choose a low calorie or vegetable-based option. If moderation, most processed or refined foods are not harmful, though because they occupy a significant part of the traditional diet, they should be avoided as much as possible.

High-Fructose Corn Syrup

One of the most insidious foods that can contribute to a lot of health conditions is high-fructose corn syrup. It is often an item that is not clearly spelled out in the ingredients list, though many box bowls of cereal, baked goods, and mixes contain this ingredient. High-fructose corn syrup differs significantly from regular sugars and sweeteners, as it contains an extraordinarily high amount of concentrated sugar. When you eat a food product containing high fructose corn syrup, your body's ability to detect fullness may be impaired, which can cause overeating. Over a long period of time, the result is obesity and negative eating habits, as eating a high sugar diet is addictive and difficult to reverse, especially when your body's ability to detect fullness is not functioning properly.

Our body can only use so much glucose at a time, even when we are active and exercise often. This means that any residual amounts are stored in the body, resulting in extra weight. Coupled with overeating, this spells a disaster for weight gain and can contribute to the development of type 2 diabetes. High-fructose corn syrup also contributes to an increased risk of liver disease, stroke, and heart disease. While some forms of natural sweeteners in moderate amounts are harmless and may even contain some nutrients, high-fructose corn syrup is void of all nutrients, and the more you consume, the less room is left for more nutrient-rich foods that your body needs.

How can you avoid HFCS (high-fructose corn syrup)? There are some easy habits to avoiding this ingredient, including avoiding anything packaged in a box or carton that is sweetened. Not every label will include the exact wording "high-fructose corn syrup," which makes it challenging to detect in some products. For this reason, it's best to become acquainted with unnatural sweeteners that may lurk in packaged foods, or avoid them completely:

- If you want to purchase hot cereals, choose raw oats on their own, and add your choice of sweeteners and ingredients, including cinnamon and maple syrup.
- Avoid all sodas and artificially sweetened beverages. Some select drinks sweetened with low carb sweeteners or natural fruit extracts may be acceptable, though always review the ingredients carefully before consuming.

- It's not just sweet foods and food products that contain HFCS. Among the products to watch for include canned tomato and pasta sauces, salad dressings, ice cream, bread, canned soups, various condiments and marinades, and many other products in cans or boxes.
- Keep your focus on the outside aisles of the grocery store, where the vast majority of foods are fresh, unpackaged, and unprocessed. If you choose a dried fruit snack, check to make sure it's sundried, which means fewer additives were used in its preparation.
- Avoid white and refined bread and baked goods, and instead choose whole grain and locally prepared goods, which list the ingredients. Bread containing flax seeds, caraway, and rye contain nutrients not found in white and refined goods.
- Skip the fruit juices, and make your own freshly squeezed juice at home. Choose tea, skim milk, coffee, and water instead.
- Avoid store-bought cookies, cakes, and pies, which are full of unnecessary sugars and additives that contribute to inflammation.

Many large-scale food product manufacturers have added some form of HFCS beginning over 40 years ago, which gives a thought to how much of an impact his additive has had on the increase of obesity and related illnesses over the past few decades. As we learn more about these products and additives, it's invaluable to making better decisions on how we select the foods and drinks we consume.

In general, avoiding as many processed foods as possible will provide a good foundation for reducing inflammation in your body and improving health overall. This may require a few slight adjustments to your current diet if you already make healthy choices during your shopping trips, or it may require a complete overhaul for a new and improved diet.

Chapter 2: The Benefits of Following an Anti-Inflammatory Diet

Health and Lifestyle Benefits of Anti-Inflammatory Foods

Once you begin to implement foods with a high nutrient level and anti-inflammatory properties, you'll notice significant benefits often within one or two weeks. If you normally experience bloating and/or inflammation, you'll notice these symptoms will reduce and may disappear altogether. Over a longer time, you may notice the benefits of weight loss, improved energy, and a reduction in symptoms from a variety of health conditions. Following an anti-inflammatory diet should not be considered a temporary fix or a quick solution, but rather a long-term commitment that fits into your lifestyle.

How do Anti-Inflammatory Foods Work?

People who tend to follow a Mediterranean diet or consume plant-based foods only will naturally alleviate stress on the body and, therefore, prevent occurrences of inflammation. This also prevents the onset of diseases and conditions that develop as we age, and help improve how we function and focus as we grow older. Regular exercise, drinking plenty of water, and avoiding processed and sugary foods are also excellent ways to prevent disease and improve overall health.

Inflammation occurs as a response to our body's immune system, as a trigger when something isn't right. When we become inflamed, it's our body's way of trying to fight an infection or condition as a natural immune response. When this happens frequently and over a longer period of time, this process becomes a trigger for other diseases and conditions, such as Alzheimer's, depression, and diabetes. It can also lead to stroke and heart disease if left untreated. Many people take medication for the treatment of inflammation, though in the long-term, it only resolves the symptoms temporarily, while further damage is done within the body. For this reason, taking a more preventative approach to your health and bodily functions is key to living the best quality of life as possible.

Focus on Healthy Nuts and Seeds

Whether your focus is eating leaner meats, including fish and poultry, or consuming a plant-based diet, all can agree that nuts and seeds should become a mainstay in your way of eating, due to the sheer number of nutrients and minerals they contain, and in such small amounts. Just a small portion of nuts and/or seeds each day can replace some vitamin supplements while providing a nutritious snack. Making these small, but mighty foods a center of your diet is a good way to make the anti-inflammatory way of eating a successful lifestyle. To become more familiar with the benefits of nuts and seeds, research as much as possible, so that you know exactly which varieties to include, not just based on nutrients, but on taste and preference.

- Almonds pack a good dose of protein, vitamin E, magnesium, and fiber. They contain very little carbohydrates and can improve cholesterol levels. In addition to having anti-inflammatory properties, almonds assist in weight loss and improving metabolism. They reduce blood pressure and improve blood sugar levels. This variety of nuts is ideal for people who have type 2 diabetes.
- Walnuts are popular and used in a lot of desserts and as a salad topping. They contain a significant amount of healthy fats and fiber, making them ideal for weight loss and maintenance. Like

almonds, they regulate blood sugar and improve metabolism, while preventing heart disease and other chronic conditions.

- Pistachios are distinguishable by their greenish color once they are removed from their shells, and are often added to desserts, puddings, and drinks, including smoothies. They make a great topping to many dishes and can also be enjoyed as a snack, roasted or raw. Pistachios help improve heart health and provide a significant amount of healthy fats for overall bodily function. Blood pressure and glucose levels are lowered, and weight loss is also improved.
- Pecans are one of the favorite nuts added to desserts, because of their pleasant texture and taste combination. They are often seen in butter tarts or pies, including ice creams and other treats. Pecans make a great snack on-the-go and provide a healthy dose of magnesium, which is essential for bone and muscle health. They are high in antioxidants and contain polyphenols, which are essentially antioxidants, which improve the quality of blood in the body while improving cholesterol levels.

- Macadamia nuts are one of the tops options for heart health, as they contain a high amount of monounsaturated fats and keep cholesterol levels normal. While they are an expensive option compared to other nut varieties, macadamia nuts can be found in bulk stores and enjoyed in small portions, as well as in recipes.
- Cashews are tasty raw or toasted, and often one of the most enjoyed snacks on their own. They are filling and make a great snack on their own, or mixed with other nuts and seeds. Metabolism and antioxidant performance have been noted in studies resulting from the consumption of cashews, as well as other nuts with similar nutrients. Cashews are high in fats and help regulate blood sugar and cholesterol.
- Brazil nuts originate from the Amazon and contain selenium, a mineral that is also an antioxidant. Deficiency in selenium can lead to a number of diseases and conditions, which makes it vital for overall health and bodily function. It helps regulate your body's weight and metabolism.
- Hazelnuts are one of the top options for spreads and additions to chocolate desserts and can be helpful in reducing the chances of heart disease.

Hazelnuts are high in vitamin E and improve the blood vessel function in the body.

- Peanuts are one of the most popular and common nuts used in recipes and everyday snacks. They are often found prepacked with salt and/or other flavors. For maximum benefits, peanuts are best consumed raw or lightly roasted, without any added salt or sugars. While they can trigger an allergic reaction for some people, they are generally safe for anyone who doesn't have any conditions impacted by peanuts. They are a good option for women who are pregnant, as regular consumption may reduce the likelihood of peanut allergies in children. This may also reduce the prevalence of childhood asthma as well. Peanut butter is another excellent option, provided no additional sugar, salt, or preservatives are added.

Seeds, like nuts, provide many health benefits and should be consumed as regularly as possible. Not all seeds may seem likely to become a part of your diet, though rotating them and trying a few varieties can give you a good idea of which ones you'd like to use more often. Some seeds are great as snacks on their own, such as sunflower or pumpkin seeds, while chia seeds, flax, and hemp seeds are used as ingredients in cereals, smoothies, and salads.

- Chia seeds are small, tiny, black or reddish-brown seeds that have become more popular in recent years due to their high levels of nutrients. Just one small serving of chia seeds contains antioxidants, protein, calcium, magnesium, omega 3 and 6s, vitamin B1, and manganese. The increased production of ALA in the blood directly reduces the prevalence of inflammation, which is the effect of chia seeds in the body. Reducing blood sugar, improving type 2 diabetes symptoms, and reducing the likelihood of heart disease are among many other benefits of chia seeds. Fortunately, you don't have to eat large amounts to reap the benefits, though a regular, small portion of your daily routine will go a long way to improving your health overall.
- Hemp seeds are an excellent source of protein and fatty acids. They contain important nutrients your body can't produce, which makes hemp an advantage to include in your diet. The quality of protein in hemp is considered high, which makes it a good option as a boost to smoothies. Some bulk stores and natural foods stores offer hemp

protein powder as a supplement for vegan bodybuilding and as a powder to add to drinks, milkshakes, and smoothies. Hemp also helps improve skin health and can fight against eczema, as well as improving the moisture levels in the skin. Some people have shown a significant decrease in eczema symptoms after regular hemp use.

- Flaxseeds are best to consume ground, rather than as whole seeds, in order to get the most out of their nutritious ingredients. High in antioxidants, fiber, and healthy fats, flaxseeds are often added to cereals, both hot and cold, to boost the nutrition value. They can also be added to smoothies like hemp and chia seeds. There are some studies that indicate possible prevention and treatment of tumors in some cases, which is promising for people who suffer from both benign and cancerous tumor growth.
- Sesame seeds are often enjoyed as a topping on desserts, bagels, bread, or stir fry dishes. They are most popular lightly toasted and can blend in with many different dishes and flavors. Some studies indicate possible prevention of heart disease and cancer due to the high level of antioxidants. They

also reduce inflammation, which provides relief from the effects of arthritis, including pain management. Consuming just a small portion of sesame seeds and/or powder each week can significantly reduce the inflammatory properties in the body. This can help improve and heal muscle stress and damage in athletes, which makes sesame powders and butter another great way to get a good dose of protein and healing properties for your body.

- Pumpkin seeds are an excellent snack on-the-go, either raw or lightly roasted, without salt. They contain phytosterols, which contribute to lower blood sugar and the likelihood of breast cancer. Pumpkin seeds have shown positive results in the treatment and prevention of both bladder and kidney stones. Prevention occurs due to the seeds' ability to lower the amount of calcium in the urine, which contributes to the formation of stones. This also has the effect of improving prostate and urinary tract function, preventing disease and infection. Women may experience relief from menopause symptoms and lowering cholesterol.
- Sunflower seeds are a tasty seed full of vitamins and healthy fats. There seems to be a significant

amount of inflammation reduction, specifically in older adults, as well as reducing heart disease and other conditions associated with inflammation. While sunflower seeds are beneficial to anyone, they are especially helpful for aging adults over the age of 50, who are prone to more chronic conditions and health issues. Other studies show promising results in post-menopausal women who have type 2 diabetes, as well as lowering and regulating cholesterol levels.

In general, unless you experience adverse reactions or severe allergies to nuts or seeds, add as many varieties as possible into your diet as a regular staple. In fact, use nuts and seeds as the centerpiece of your diet and build your fruits, vegetables, and meat or vegan proteins around them. Making nuts and seeds the focus of your diet has many benefits in itself, for more reasons than health:

- Nuts and seeds are portable and can be easily added to any dishes at home or on the go.
- While some nuts and seeds are expensive, many can be purchased in bulk, making them easier to control in terms of portion and consumption. This will help you plan your budget around the foods you eat, to include portions and costs.

- They are easy as a snack and when you are in a crunch for a meal. If you don't have time for breakfast in the morning or might skip a meal at the point in the day, a handful of nuts and/or seeds can fill the gap until you have the chance to enjoy a full meal.
- Yogurt, oatmeal, salads, and smoothies are just some of the foods you can add nuts and seeds too, even when you don't have time to make them at home. For example, a take-out salad from the local restaurant or café near work can easily be topped with a few teaspoons of chia seeds, pistachios, and/or peanuts.

Chapter 3: Smoothies and Beverages

Smoothies (Dairy and Plant-based)

Smoothies and milkshakes are a great meal replacement option or treatment that can provide a quick boost. They can make an excellent snack before a workout at the gym or bicycle ride. There are many options for smoothies, including the types of base you choose, such as milk (dairy, coconut, almond, and other nut-based milk), tea, or juice. Most often, juice or milk is combined with a handful of ingredients and supplements to "boost" the nutrient content. Some people may enjoy smoothies or milkshakes as a dessert, though you can include a lot of healthy ingredients to suit any occasion.

Note: The smoothie recipes below offer a variety of sweetener options (either natural, unprocessed, or low carb) and focus on non-dairy milk as options, to include as many non-inflammatory foods as possible. You may substitute non-dairy milk with skim milk or another low-fat dairy option. Soymilk can also be used, as well as other non-dairy milk not mentioned, depending on your preference. Some of the smoothies include yogurt, which can be dairy (low fat and unsweetened) or a plant-based variety, such as coconut cultured yogurt or soy-based products.

Avocado and Coconut Milk Smoothie

Avocados are naturally high in good fats, which make them ideal for any meal, including smoothies. When they are very ripe, they make an excellent addition to dips, smoothies, and as a spread over toast. They can be easily added to other ingredients in a blender to create many delicious concoctions, one of which is easy and requires only three ingredients:

- 1 large ripened avocado (at room temperature)
- 1 ½ cups of coconut milk
- 2-3 teaspoons honey, maple syrup, or a low carb sweetener (Swerve or monk fruit)

Combine all ingredients in a blender and pulse until smooth. Continue to blend on medium or high speed until the texture is even. If the mixture is too thick and difficult to pour into a glass, add more coconut milk. To chill, add ice and blend. This recipe makes one or two servings.

Banana and Avocado Smoothie

Another option for avocado in a smoothie includes adding a banana with either almond or coconut milk. If desired, add soy or another nut-based milk instead (vanilla flavored is suggested).

- 1 large ripened avocado
- 1 ripe banana
- 1 ½ cups almond or coconut milk
- 2-3 teaspoons of natural or low carb sweetener

Blend the ingredients until smooth. If there are any lumps, pulse, then blend until the smoothie is even and serve.

Berries and Bananas Smoothie

Combining berries and bananas provides a tasty treat for breakfast as a treat. Berries have a natural sweetness of their own, and often don't require any additional sweeteners. Bananas are rich in potassium and fiber, which reduce water retention and provide about 90 minutes of energy in just one serving. Berries are delicious and contain vitamin C, and while they contain natural sugar (fructose), they are easily digested and support a nutritious diet. Choose any variety of berries, either on their own or in combination:

strawberries, raspberries, blueberries, blackberries, and cherries.

- 1 ripe banana
- 1 ½ - 2 cups coconut or almond milk
- ½ - 1 cups of berries (any choice or combination)
- 2-3 teaspoons of natural or low carb sweetener (optional)

Combine all ingredients in a blender and mix well. Berries can be frozen or fresh, though if frozen, blend longer to ensure they don't leave lumps behind. To chill the smoothie, add one or two ice cubes, and blend or slice a banana into small pieces and freeze ahead before adding. Makes one or two servings.

Pumpkin Spice Smoothie

Pumpkins are a healthy, fiber-filled fruit that goes beyond pumpkin pie and muffins. Fresh or canned pureed pumpkin is an excellent source of vitamins A and C, with a low amount of sugar and high fiber. It blends well with any variety of milk, either dairy or non-dairy.

- ½ cup or 1/3 can of pumpkin puree
- 1 ½ cups of coconut or almond milk
- 2-3 teaspoons of natural or low carb sweetener

- 1 tablespoon pumpkin spice, or combine 1 teaspoon of each: cinnamon, nutmeg, and ¼ teaspoon cloves

Blend the pumpkin puree and milk first, then add the sweetener and spices, continuing to mix until smooth. If you find the sweetness isn't adequate, add more honey, maple syrup, or your choice of low carb sweetener to enhance the flavor. Another option to consider is adding half a ripe banana or 2 teaspoons of crushed pistachios. Makes one or two servings.

Mangos, Bananas, and Peaches Smoothie

Combining these three fruits can provide a unique blend of fruits. If you choose frozen peaches and/or mangoes, add more milk or juice as a base so they blend easier. Adding milk as the base will create a thicker smoothie than a juice, and may require a bit of sweetener unless you are satisfied with the natural sugars in the fruits. Fresh peaches, when in season, are the best option, as well as mangoes. If only one of these options is available, double the amount for this recipe.

- 1 ripe banana
- 2 cups coconut or almond milk
- 1 small peach, pitted, skin removed and sliced

- 1 small or medium-sized mango, pitted, skin removed and sliced
- 1-2 teaspoons natural sweetener, honey or maple syrup (optional)

Blend the ingredients and mix until smooth. If the smoothie is too thick, add more milk to thin until the desired consistency is achieved. To add juice as a base for this smoothie, use the following:

- 1 ripe banana
- 2 cups freshly squeezed orange juice (or pineapple juice)
- 1 small peach, pitted, skin removed and sliced
- 1 small or medium-sized mango, pitted, skin removed and sliced
- 1-2 teaspoons sweetener (optional)

Combine the ingredients in a blender and mix until smooth. You may choose to add the sweetener after mixing the other ingredients first to avoid adding too much. Freshly squeezed and unsweetened orange juice is recommended and will likely contain enough sugar for this recipe on its own. Makes two servings.

Pineapple and Coconut Smoothie

Closely resembling a Pina Colada drink, this smoothie combines the tropical flavors of pineapple and coconut for a tasty beverage. Coconut milk is the best option for this drink, though it can be made with another milk along with a dash of coconut cream or powder (unsweetened).

- 1 cup of fresh, sliced pineapple (or frozen chunks of pineapple)
- 1 ½ cups of coconut milk
- ½ teaspoon vanilla
- 2-3 teaspoons sweetener
- Dash of cinnamon (optional)
- Dash of cocoa powder (optional)

Combine all ingredients and mix well in a blender. Frozen pineapple will take longer to integrate with the other items and may take longer. Other options to consider for this recipe include adding half a ripe banana (or one whole banana), a few frozen chunks of mango, and/or papaya for a more tropical flavor. Adjust the sweetness level to your preference. Makes one or two servings.

Kefir and Berries Smoothie

Kefir is a fermented drink like yogurt, which contains a higher amount of probiotics and nutrients that contribute to good gut health. Promoting a healthy gut and bacterial balance is key to preventing a lot of inflammation, which is triggered by infections and conditions affecting the gut. This smoothie is a great option for strengthening the microbial balance in your body. Kefir has grown in popularity, and while it used to be only available in natural food stores, it can often be found in the dairy section of most grocery stores. It tastes like yogurt, only slightly thinner in texture, which makes it ideal for creating smoothies.

- 2 cups of kefir (unsweetened, unflavored)
- 1 cup mixed berries (frozen or fresh)
- 2-3 teaspoons of low carb sweetener

Combine all ingredients in the blender and pulse until smooth. If the berries are frozen, they may take longer to blend. For best results, thaw the berries until they are nearly thawed, but chilled enough to keep the smoothie cold. If the smoothie is too thick, add ½-1 cup of coconut or almond milk, or skim milk.

Options for this smoothie include adding half a banana, or fresh mango or peach. This recipe makes two servings.

Hot and Cold Drinks

There are a variety of beverages to reduce inflammation. Coffee and many varieties of tea are high in antioxidants, and when enjoyed daily, they can offer many benefits for your health, including the prevention of various diseases and conditions. Green tea has grown in popularity, especially the Sencha and Matcha varieties, which are offered in many restaurants and grocery stores. Many hot drinks can be simply brewed or steeped in water, while others can be whipped up with a skim or non-diary milk as a base. Cold drinks can be an iced version of warm drinks or a refreshing glass of freshly squeezed citrus juice (orange, lemon, lime, grapefruit) with a dash of natural sweetener.

Freshly Brewed Coffee

It's simple, easy to make, and helps you start your day each morning. If you brew your coffee at home, consider purchasing a grinder for coffee beans, so they can be freshly ground each morning just before brewing. This will provide a fresher, tastier cup of java to enjoy. Also, consider the following when selecting coffee beans to improve the quality and taste:

- Purchase from a locally-sourced or fair-trade supplier of coffee. This is both an ethical shopping choice, as well as a healthier one, as the beans are often of better quality when they are purchased fair-trade.
- Choose organic beans or coffee that has not been subjected to pesticides or similar treatments. Not only does the quality of organic beans make a difference in the taste, but they are also more beneficial to your overall health
- Avoid pre-ground coffee beans, unless you don't have a grinder at home. If you have your beans ground on-site, either in a local shop or grocery store, seal them in a bag and prevent re-opening until they are to be used to preserve their freshness.

Coffee is versatile in that it can be served as a simple "drip" cup or as a fancier beverage, such as a latte, cappuccino, or an americano. When you enjoy your java, avoid using too much sugar, if at all, and instead consider adding honey, raw (unprocessed) sugar, or a low carb option, such as Swerve. If you enjoy your coffee with cream or milk, consider a low-fat option, such as skim milk, or a dairy-free alternative, such as soy or coconut-based creamers. As more non-dairy milk and beverages become popular, you'll notice a wide variety in grocery stores to choose from, including different flavors, such as vanilla and chocolate.

What are the health benefits of coffee? There are plenty and account for some of the reasons why people enjoy coffee as their favorite beverage, which is one of the most consumed drinks around the world. Aside from waking you up in the morning, there are many other reasons to enjoy a tasty cup of coffee:

- Reduces sensation of pain, and in some people, it can reduce pain associated with chronic headaches.
- Lowers the risk of memory loss and other related conditions, such as Parkinson's and Alzheimer's disease
- Enhances mood and reduces the effects of depression
- Reduces the risk of heart disease, liver damage, and type 2 diabetes
- Increases the amount of fiber in your diet

If you experience conditions that can be irritated by coffee or caffeine in general, it may be best to avoid or limit your consumption of this beverage. While it is a safe drink, it can cause flare-ups for people who suffer from IBS (irritable bowel syndrome) or heartburn. As you adapt to an anti-inflammatory diet, you may find that many symptoms and flare-ups subside, which can make it easier to enjoy foods and drinks you may have previously avoided, including coffee.

Iced Coffee

If you didn't have the time to finish your morning coffee, you could easily convert the day's leftover brew into an iced treat. Iced coffee is popular during the warmer months, though can be made any time of the day or year. It's refreshing and can be spiced, sweetened, or simply enjoyed as is (black or with a little milk and/or sweetener).

Hot Chocolate

Most packaged brands of hot chocolate are full of sugar and additives, which makes them a poor choice. However, this tasty treat can be made easily at home by melting dark baker's chocolate or cocoa powder with skim or non-dairy milk and a bit of sweetener. The number of ingredients can be adjusted to suit your preference, and you may want to try different types of milk, such as hazelnut, coconut, or soy, to test which version of non-dairy milk works best for you.

Mocha

Combining hot chocolate with leftover coffee or a freshly brewed cup is a nice twist on both beverages. This drink is often enjoyed with a dollop of whipped cream, which can be dairy or a coconut-based product.

Ginger and Cardamom Drink

Coconut milk is based used to prepare this drink, which features a generous helping of cardamom and ginger spices.

- 2 cups of coconut milk
- 2 tablespoons cardamom spice
- 1 tablespoon ginger spice
- 2 tablespoons low carb sweetener

In a small saucepan, heat the coconut milk. Using a whisk, add the sweetener, cardamom, and ginger. Whisk slowly until heated, though avoid boiling. If you want to enhance the ginger flavor, add more powder or a ginger tea bag. Serve warm in a mug and top with nutmeg or cinnamon.

Turmeric Spice Drink

Prepared like the ginger and cardamom drink, this includes coconut milk. If desired, almond milk or skim milk can be used instead, though coconut milk is featured because of it's thick, creamy texture and mild flavor. Turmeric is one of the best natural treatments against inflammation and offers a pleasant taste, as well.

- 2 cups of coconut milk
- 2-3 tablespoons turmeric spice
- ½ teaspoon black pepper
- 2 tablespoons low carb sweetener

In a small saucepan, heat the coconut milk. Add the sweetener and turmeric and whisk together, then add the black pepper. Continue to heat and stir, then serve warm and top with a dash of turmeric.

Freshly Squeezed Juices

If you own a juicer, it's a great appliance that can be put to good use for natural fruit and vegetable juices. There are a variety of tasty combinations to try, which feature distinct flavors and nutrients. Before you select the ingredients for your juice, consider the benefits of some of the most popular options:

- Kale and spinach: high in calcium, protein, and fiber. These are leafy greens that help prevent cancer and fight against chronic conditions, such as arthritis. They contain many vitamins as well.
- Cucumber is made of water and works well as a means of detoxing your liver and kidneys, helping to improve their function.
- Carrots and celery: these are both often used as side snacks or as part of a vegetable platter, and they can work well in a juice too! Carrots contain beta carotene, which is good for your vision, as well as many vitamins, such as A and K. Celery is a good source of vitamins C, A, and K, and both vegetables are high in fiber.
- Beets are high in iron and help reduce blood pressure and support the liver.

- Ginger is excellent for the prevention of common colds, boosting the immune system's function, and promotes good gut health, including digestion.
- Other good options include citrus fruits, apples, and turmeric.

Turmeric is one of the best foods for reducing inflammation, and it is recommended to use it as often as possible as a spice, supplement, or ingredient in a juice or meal. Using turmeric often, along with other anti-inflammatory foods, can go a long way to preventing conditions and discomfort with inflammation. Turmeric contains antioxidants that help prevent cancer.

If you're new to juicing, the following combinations are suggested for tasting various fruits together. Ensure your juicer is always cleaned after each use and that all foods are fresh or freshly thawed if you keep them frozen. Try "testing" small portions at a time, in case you want to change the portion and/or choices. For example, start with a mild assortment of flavors, such as carrots and orange, and eventually introduce stronger flavors, such as spinach, kale, then ginger and beets. The following combinations are popular and often used together in juicing:

- Carrot and orange juice

- Mango and carrot juice
- Kale, spinach, and orange juice
- Beets and ginger juice
- Lemon, turmeric, and ginger juice

Chapter 4: Soups and Stews

A hearty soup or stew on a cold day can be a delicious and wholesome way to warm up and get the nutrients you need to prevent illness and inflammation. Many stews are easy to make, though they can take a while to prepare.

Light Soups and Broths

Often considered an appetizer or starter, a small portion or light soups can be a wonderful addition to the main meal as aside.

Bone Broth

Preparation time: 30 minutes

Cooking time: 20-24 hours

Makes 6-8 servings

Due to the surge in popularity of low carb diets, bone broth has become a popular supplement either in powder form or as a meal replacement. Bone broth is an excellent source of collagen and protein and can be consumed during periods of fasting, which is practiced with intermittent fasting or longer time frames. Adding just a cup of bone broth to your diet, at least twice or three times each week, can strengthen your muscles and bones, support your immune system against conditions and weakening joints that cause chronic pain.

How do you make bone broth? For many people who consume broth regularly, they choose to purchase the powdered form of broth for easy preparation: simply boil a cup of water and stir in the broth mix. Varieties and flavors range from chicken and beef to more enhanced combinations of mushroom and beef, for example, or a variety of spices may be added, such as chili powder, turmeric, and lemongrass among others. A quick search online will provide many variations available for purchase in cartons, tins, and portable single-portion packets.

If you choose to make bone broth from scratch, it requires very few ingredients and a lot of time. Select a time frame that allows for a minimum of 24-hours to prepare, boil, and simmer your broth for 20-24 hours. This is the recommended timeframe required for bones to transfer their nutrients into the water to form a broth. If you don't have any leftover roast beef, chicken, or turkey, you can visit a local butcher to purchase bones.

It's recommended that bones are obtained from grass-fed, locally raised cattle or poultry for best results and high quality. You'll find that many high-quality bone broths prepared for stores feature grass-fed and naturally raised beef or chicken, and this should be taken into consideration when preparing from scratch.

Once you have the bones or have removed them from a leftover chicken or beef roast, transfer them to a large cooking pot and fill between two thirds or three-quarters with water, including the bones. This will allow enough space on top when the broth begins to boil. If the bones have some meat and/or pieces of fat attached, this can be included, if it is your preference, or you can clean the bones completely and only include them in the preparation of the broth. Bring the water and bones to a boil, then cover, reduce heat to low-medium, and continue to simmer.

What can you add to bone broth? Salt is the most common ingredient, though if you are aiming to reduce salt to improve your health, keep the amount minimal, or choose sea salt or pink Himalayan salt. There are suitable alternatives that can provide a similar "salty" taste if avoidance is the goal. Turmeric is highly recommended for its high nutrient levels and effects on reducing inflammation. Add as much or as little as desired. Other ingredients to consider include chili pepper, cayenne, and black pepper. If you add any additional spices or flavors to enhance the broth, you can do this at any time during the cooking process, preferably halfway through, when the bones have enriched the water and there remains time to stew the spices with the broth. More can be added towards the end once the broth is drained into a second, smaller pot and the bones are removed. Broth can be frozen or refrigerated and consumed over the next three or four days.

Miso Soup

Preparation and cooking time: 20 minutes

Makes 2-3 servings

An excellent plant-based alternative to bone broth, miso soup is common in sushi restaurants and offered in many grocery and natural food stores. Miso is fermented soy, which takes anywhere from several weeks to months or even years, depending on the strength and flavor desired. The best way to prepare miso soup is to select a brand of paste or dried varieties in your local grocery store and try the different types of miso pastes available:

- White miso is the mildest and often favored by many people looking for a subtle, pleasant taste. This type of miso is prepared with rice and soybeans and usually takes several weeks to ferment, which is a relatively short period of time compared to other varieties of miso. White miso is known as Shiro miso. Many recipes may include this type of miso as part of a marinade or dressing, though its most commonly used in soup.
- Yellow miso is stronger than the white variety. If you enjoy white miso and looking for more flavor, this may be a good option. This variety is known as Shinshu miso and is used in the same way white miso is applied, though most often as a soup or as part of a marinade. Yellow miso is prepared by fermenting barley with soybeans, and this is usually done for a longer period of time, usually several months.
- Red miso is salty and delivers a powerful taste in a small pinch. It's known as Aka Miso and is fermented the longest of the three main varieties, for months, possibly a year or more. The process involves fermenting barley with other grains and soybeans. Some varieties may appear brown in color or reddish-brown. While red miso can be

used in soups, it's a better option for topping meat dishes as a glaze or condiment, as well as roasted or stewed vegetables.

How is miso soup prepared? Most packages provide easy instructions. Like store-bought bone broth, simply boil water and add a specified amount and stir. Add a little at first and test taste to determine if more is needed. Miso soup is tasty on its own, or it can be enhanced by adding some of the following ingredients:

- Dried seaweed
- Firm tofu, sliced into small cubes
- Sliced green onion
- Parsley
- Black pepper
- Chili pepper

Miso naturally contains salt, which makes it ideal without adding any extra as a condiment. If you need to avoid or reduce sodium in your diet, use white and yellow varieties of miso. The longer the miso is fermented during the preparation process, the stronger the taste.

Consommé Soups

Preparation time: 60 minutes

Total cooking and preparation time: 3 hours

Makes 2-4 servings

Popular in French cuisine, consommé soups are prepared like bone broth by boiling the bones to create a stock, then adding more ingredients, such as tomato, basil leaves or similar herbs, and egg whites. This can be varied depending on the specific recipe followed, and the spices and/or herbs can be switched according to personal taste and preference. The following recipe (chicken consommé soup) is easy if you are new to this type of soup, which is a great light meal or served with grilled or lightly sautéed vegetables:

- Bones of one chicken
- 1 medium onion, chopped, with the skin attached
- 2-3 teaspoons of dried tarragon
- 2-3 teaspoons dried parsley
- 3 large egg whites
- 2-3 bay leaves
- Dash of black pepper
- 1 large carrot, chopped
- 1 large celery stalk, chopped

- 2 large garlic cloves, chopped, with skin attached

Prepare a large cooking pot with the bones of one chicken and fill three-quarters. Add all ingredients (except the eggs) and bring to a boil. Gently reduce heat and continue to boil for another 1 ½ to 2 hours. Reduce heat and cook longer, if desired, for another hour until the flavor is strong. Taste test often, then drain all the ingredients and transfer the liquid to a second pot and return to the stovetop to simmer for a few more minutes, stirring during this process. Remove from heat and refrigerate for 2-3 hours, then remove any fat accumulated on the surface of the soup. In a medium bowl, whisk the egg whites, then add and stir into the consommé. Return to the stovetop and bring to a boil, until the egg whites float on top of the soup. Gently remove the egg whites on top and take caution not to mix them into the soup, as this will cause it to become cloudy. Once this process is done, the soup will become clear and can be served immediately or refrigerated until served later.

Options of consommé soup include adding cherry tomatoes, fennel sprouts, and a variety of other herbs and spices just before serving. This light soup is excellent to serve with anti-inflammatory vegetables such as baked squash, yams, or zucchini.

Hearty Stews and Chili

Stews and chili dishes provide a lot of warmth and comfort during the colder months of the year or serve as a delicious meal that can last over several days. While the lighter varieties of soups are suitable for a refreshing, warm treat, these dishes are heartier and provide a complete meal within one serving. These are not only excellent for your health, but they also tend to be easier on the budget, providing a lot of nutrients in small doses, which means they last for second and third servings. A large batch of stew or chili can be prepared for a duration of up to one week.

Lean Beef Chili

Preparation time: 60 minutes

Cooking time: 1-2 hours

Makes 6-8 servings

Choosing lean red meat is an excellent option for chili, and only a small amount is needed for a large serving. Extra-lean cuts of beef or ground beef work well with this recipe. If you purchase the meat frozen, allow it to thaw overnight and chill in the refrigerator until ready. To further enhance the flavor before cooking the chili, marinate in the following mix of spices and ingredients:

- 2 large cans of tomato sauce
- 1 pound of extra-lean ground beef (if not available, lean ground beef is a good option)
- 2 teaspoons of basil
- 2 teaspoons of oregano
- Salt and black pepper
- 2-3 crushed cloves of garlic
- 1 small onion, finely sliced
- 1 small can of tomato paste
- 1-2 cups of water or tomato juice (optional, may be used to keep the chili moist, prevent drying)
- 1 stalk of celery, chopped
- 1 can of black beans
- 1 can of chickpeas
- 1 can of kidney beans
- ½ can of pinto beans
- 2-3 tablespoons chili powder
- 1-2 teaspoons cayenne pepper

Heat a skillet on medium heat and add olive oil to coat. Add the lean ground beef and cook until brown, then add crushed garlic, onions, salt (optional), and black pepper. Continue to fry for another 5-6 minutes, then remove from heat. Prepare a large cooking pot by adding both cans of tomato, then add all the beans, cooked ground beef, and spices. Cook on medium heat until bubbling, then reduce heat to low-medium or low so that the chili will not burn. Stir periodically every 10-15 minutes and taste test after one hour. Add more spices, garlic, and/or tomato sauce, and other ingredients as desired to achieve the exact flavor you want. If the mixture becomes too thick, slowly add water and/or some tomato juice. Continue to cook until the beans are soft and serve topped with sliced jalapenos and/or shredded cheese.

All ingredients in this recipe are anti-inflammatory, though adding extra salt and topping with cheese may slightly increase the chances of triggering a flare-up. If you want to avoid this possibility, add vegan cheese, skim milk cheese, or crumbled feta cheese (goat cheese) in place of the cheddar cheese. Any type of beans can be substituted for more of one variety or omitted altogether if desired.

Enjoy chili as a meal for lunch, dinner, or as a small side with poached or scrambled eggs for breakfast. This dish can easily serve 4-6 people and may provide second or third servings, depending on the portion size and additional food served alongside the chili. Leftover portions can also be served over the bread as hot sandwiches or with a low-calorie pasta or baked spaghetti squash.

Lean Beef Stew

Preparation time: 60 minutes

Cooking time: 1-2 hours

Makes 6-8 servings

A hearty meal on its own, lean beef stew is great with whole-grain bread high in fiber and full of seeds. There are many options for ingredients for this recipe, depending on your preferences, which may include adding barley, quinoa, and/or rice or more vegetables, such as zucchini, carrots, spinach, onions, and potatoes. This meal can be prepared mild or spicy or somewhere in between. Preparing the broth can be done by using all the bones from a leftover roast and preparing as the bone broth, or by adding 1 large or 2 medium cartons of prepared beef broth (approximately 3 cups). Choose a low sodium option of broth or prepare your own with little or no salt.

This recipe contains a lot of ingredients, and many of the spices can be adjusted according to personal preference. As with other stews and soups, a teaspoon or two of turmeric is recommended to boost the anti-inflammatory properties of this meal. If needed, use turmeric in place of salt, as the beef broth will likely contain enough sodium for the recipe.

- 2 teaspoons of olive oil
- Dash of salt (optional)
- 1-2 teaspoons of dried turmeric
- 2 pounds of stewing beef, chopped into cubes
- 1 teaspoon of paprika
- 1 teaspoon of basil
- 1 teaspoon of thyme
- 1 teaspoon of chili powder (optional)
- 2 tablespoons of flour (all-purpose flour works best)
- 2 cloves of garlic, crushed
- 1 medium onion, chopped finely
- 2 medium-sized carrots, chopped
- 1-2 stalks of celery, chopped
- 1 teaspoon of Worcestershire sauce
- ½ cup of wine (red preferred – this is optional)
- 1/3 cups of tomato sauce
- 2 teaspoons of tomato paste
- 3 cups of beef stock (prepared or store-bought)
- 1 cup of green beans
- 3-4 potatoes, chopped into small cubes

Prepare a large stewing pot for the stovetop and combine the beef broth, 2 pounds of stewing beef, salt, and pepper and bring to a boil. Maintain the boil for a few minutes and carefully stew the beef, then reduce to medium and continue to cook until the beef is well done. Add the tomato sauce and paste first until evenly mixed with the broth and beef, then add the vegetables, including the garlic, onion, celery, carrots, potatoes, and green beans. Continue to stir and add small amounts of water if needed. Pour in the flour continuing to stir slowly, then the spices, and continue to stir for a few minutes, then cover and cook on low-medium for another hour. Check the stew every 20 minutes and stir periodically to ensure all ingredients cook and mix evenly. After an hour, taste and add more spices as desired. Serve in small bowls as a side or a large full-meal entrée with a side of multi-grain bread.

Beef stew will last for at least one week in the refrigerator and often tastes stronger the following day due to it marinating longer in the beef broth and juices. If you enjoy making stew often and would like to consider variations to this recipe, consider the following options:

- Substitute the beef broth and stewing beef for chicken broth and boneless chicken breast. To prepare the meat, bake in the oven or lightly boil so that the chicken is at least partially cooked before adding to the stew.

- If you make chicken stew, adding rice, okra, and zucchini are tasty options to consider.
- Add tomato juice with ground beef in place of the stewed beef. This can be easily adapted into a pasta stew, low carb or low-calorie noodles, or a variety of vegetables.

Chapter 5: Sides, Snacks, and Salads

Fresh, Homemade Salads

Salads are often considered as a side dish or appetizer, often as a garden, Greek or Caesar salad, and little else. Fortunately, there is an entire world of recipes that center around salads and leafy green bases for any meal type. A salad can serve as a side or a complete meal on its own, including nuts, seeds, dried fruits, cooked meats, seafood, and a variety of vegetables. Toppings and dressings and limitless, and the combination of ingredients can be simple, complex, and customized.

Building a salad begins with a base, which is traditionally a leafy green, such as lettuce, cabbage, kale, spinach, or arugula. While all options are healthy, a dark leafy vegetable is ideal for maximizing the nutrient levels for overall health. Preparing the greens by slicing the leaves into bite-size pieces or slicing into strips. If you choose kale, remove the stems first before slicing the leaves. Some varieties of kale have a tougher, thicker texture to work with, which makes their preparation for any meal important, especially if served raw as in a salad. It's important to slice kale in small pieces that are easy to combine with other ingredients.

Which variety of kale is best to use in a salad? All the kale is good! It's helpful to become familiar with the different varieties, as they each contain different colors and textures, some of which may be preferred for a specific dish or meal.

Types of Kale, Spinach, and Arugula

The focus for salads will be on three greens, all dark, leafy green, and contain some of the highest amounts of nutrients for the best results for reducing symptoms associated with many health conditions, including inflammation. Maintaining a regular amount of dark greens in your diet will ensure steady prevention and reduction in inflammation, and while these vegetables tend to be bitter to taste, they can be marinated, coated, and flavored with other ingredients to make them tastier and compliment the bitter with sweet and tangy.

Types of Kale

Kale is a hardy vegetable that can grow in harsh climates and survive through many different types of climate. It's also available in a variety of textures and colors:

- Curly kale is a popular variety and usually commonly available in grocery stores and fresh markets when it's in season. The texture is fibrous and curly, which makes it challenging to prepare for salads. However, it holds also flavor and marinates well because of the texture, which is a major advantage. It's light to medium green in color.
- Redbor Kale, also simply called red kale, is usually curly in texture and deep purplish-red in color. The texture is nearly identical to curly kale.
- Jacinto kale is the most common variety in grocery stores. The leaves are thin and have a smooth surface, which makes it easier to slice and separate the stems for meal preparation. Also known as dinosaur kale, because of its tall, narrow shape, it's an adaptable variety that grows well in cold weather.
- Black kale is less common, though it may appear in some markets and grocery stores, depending on its availability locally. It's usually like the Jacinto kale in texture, smoother, and easy to work with.

Other types of kale include premier kale, Siberian, Red Russian, and Kamome red kale, including many other types that may be more available in some regions more than others. If you reside in a region with cooler seasons and interested in using kale in a variety of salads and meals, it may be worthwhile to research the different varieties native to your specific region and when they are in season.

Once your preferred kale is chosen, it's important to prepare it for the meal. When kale is cooked, it softens and becomes easier to eat and enjoy with other ingredients. In salads, it is often raw and can be lightly coated in a variety of dressings or drizzled in oil or vinaigrette. Keep in mind that curly textured kale will hold flavors and other ingredients better because of its shape, while smoother varieties are easier to slice.

Types of Spinach

There are over twenty types of spinach, though several are most common and the varieties you'll likely notice in your salad or meals. The three most frequently grown and cultivated spinach types include the following:

- Smooth leaf spinach is the most popular. If there is only one type of spinach in your local grocery store, it's likely this type. This variety is easy to clean, slice, and cook. It's often found frozen in grocery stores.

- Savoy spinach refers to a more textured, "crinkled" type of leaves that are challenging to clean and prepare for meals, though they can be a good addition to salads, much like curly kale.
- Semi-savoy spinach is less textured than the savoy variety, while not completely smooth either. It's like a hybrid of the first two varieties.

Types of Arugula

There are two distinct varieties of arugula you're most likely to come across. They are often referred to as the "rocket" and can grow annually in Mediterranean regions. The two most popular types of arugula are as follows:

- Wild arugula is considered a more pungent, spicy-flavored variety. It can be used in cooking and as an ingredient in sandwiches and wraps.
- Cultivated arugula is milder by comparison to the wild version of this plant and used in the same way. It's ideal for salads, as well as sandwiches, wraps, and as a garnish.

Spinach, arugula, and other greens are also high in nutrients, though kale is one of the highest and can be combined with other greens as well. When choosing your salad base, keep in mind the level of nutrients and types of vitamins and minerals each contains to customize your diet. Dark green vegetables contain a significant about of iron and calcium, which can supplement or replace meat in some or all of your diet.

Kale Salad with Blueberries and Goat Cheese

Preparation time: 20 minutes

Makes 2-4 servings

This salad combines the tangy, sweetness of blueberries with the richness of goat cheese and textured bitter flavor of kale. The ingredients are easy to find, though farro, a grain that resembles puffed rice, may be challenging to spot in your local grocery store. If you can't locate farro, substitute with quinoa or couscous.

- 1 cup of farro (or substitute with quinoa or couscous), uncooked
- Dash of sea salt
- ¾ cups of raw slivered or sliced almonds
- ½ cups of dried or fresh blueberries
- 4 ounces of goat cheese
- 1 bunch of curly kale (or any variety of kale)

Salad dressing:

- ¼ cups of olive oil (extra virgin)
- 2 teaspoons of red wine vinegar
- 2 cloves of garlic
- Dash of sea salt
- 1 teaspoon of mustard (Dijon is recommended)

In a medium cooking pot, prepare the farro (or couscous or quinoa) by cooking until soft and ready. If you are using dried blueberries, add them to the grain while it's just about finished cooking so that they become slightly fuller, then remove from heat. While the grains are cooking, prepare the kale by removing the stems and slicing in small, bite sizes, then combine both the cooked grains (when finished, then drained) with the chopped kale in a medium or large bowl. Add in the berries as well (dried or fresh). Combine well, then heat a skillet on the stovetop and lightly toast the almonds, stirring frequently on medium until they are toasted, though not burnt. Once they are golden in color, remove from heat and top the salad. Prepare the salad dressing in a small bowl by combining all ingredients and set aside. Slowly pour the dressing over the salad, and mix gently, making sure all ingredients are coated evenly. Crumble the goat cheese on top and serve.

Variations to this recipe to consider include the following:

- Substitute the blueberries for cranberries (fresh or dried) or cherries (dried)
- Use rice instead of couscous, quinoa, or farro
- Add a splash of freshly squeezed lemon or orange to the salad dressing
- Substitute goat cheese with plant-based cheese, to make the dish vegan
- Substitute almonds with pecans or walnuts, either raw or toasted and drizzled in honey

Kale, Quinoa, and Black Bean Salad

Preparation time: 20 minutes

Makes 2-4 servings

This salad creates a meal on its own. The ingredients resemble several sides, which combine into one dish that can be enjoyed for brunch, lunch, or dinner. There are a lot of nutrients in addition to the kale, which includes sweet potatoes, avocado, black beans, and feta cheese.

- 1 can of black beans
- ½ cup of crumbled feta cheese
- 1/3 cups of pumpkin seeds
- 1 cup of quinoa

- 1 bunch of kale (any variety)
- 2 limes, juiced
- Dash of sea salt
- 6 tablespoons of olive oil, divided into three portions of 2 tablespoons each
- 2 medium sweet potatoes or yams, diced into small cubes
- 2 teaspoons of ground cumin
- 1 teaspoon of paprika
- 2 medium avocados, ripe, but still firm, sliced lengthwise (pitted and peeled)
- 1 teaspoon of ground coriander
- Cilantro leaves for garnish and for the sauce (one bunch in total)
- 1 sliced jalapeno (diced finely) – optional

To prepare the salad, consider it as a collection of three sides: sweet potatoes/yams, avocados, quinoa, and kale. Cook the quinoa on the stovetop until ready, then drain and set aside. In a skillet, heat two tablespoons of olive oil on medium heat and add the sweet potatoes, then add cumin, paprika, and salt. Sauté until potatoes soften, then add 2-3 tablespoons of water and continue to cook on low-medium heat, until tender, then remove from heat. In a large bowl, prepare the kale by removing the stems, then slice the leaves into small bite-size portions. Toss in the bowl with two tablespoons of olive oil, lime juice and a dash of sea salt. Make sure all pieces of kale are evenly coated with all the ingredients.

There are now three bowls or pots with sides: sweet potatoes, quinoa, and kale. To prepare the dressing, add the avocado, the juice from two limes, jalapenos, coriander, cilantro, two tablespoons of olive oil, and a dash of salt to a blender or food processor and pulse until smooth. Combine the quinoa and kale in one bowl, and top over the sweet potatoes in another bowl, then add in the black beans, avocado sauce, and crumbled feta cheese (optional). Serve in small bowls or as a main dish.

Variations to this salad include the following:

- Skip the feta cheese to change this salad vegan
- Add couscous instead of quinoa or rice
- Sprinkle with toasted sesame seeds instead of goat cheese (or in addition to the cheese)

Kale and Tahini Salad

Preparation time: 25 minutes

Makes 2-4 servings

Tahini is a nutritious nut-based butter made from sesame seeds and is often overlooked as an option in many dishes, including salads and spreads. This salad is versatile, in that it doesn't require a specific list of ingredients, but rather, any items you have left at your disposal that will create a tasty salad with kale and tahini. The following options may be considered (and included) in this "create-your-own-salad-with-kale-and-tahini" adventure:

- Thinly sliced carrots (raw) or sliced as slivers or spirals
- Spiral sliced zucchini, squash, and/or sweet potato
- Leftover rice, couscous, barley, rice, quinoa, or any other cooked grains available and left from a previous meal
- Sliced avocado (firm, slightly ripe)
- Dried fruits such as cherries, raisins, cranberries, etc.
- Walnuts, pecans, pumpkin seeds (raw or toasted), almonds, cashews, pistachios, etc.
- Sliced apples and/or pear

Combine any or all the above, including any other ingredients you find and want to add to this dish. To create the salad dressing, the following items can be combined and blended:

- 3 tablespoons of tahini (softened, at room temperature)
- 2 teaspoons honey or maple syrup
- ¼ cups of olive oil
- ¼ cups of lime juice
- 1 bunch of Cilantro (fresh)
- ¼ teaspoon dried cumin
- 1 teaspoon chili pepper
- 1 small jalapeno pepper, thinly sliced
- 1 crushed garlic clove

Combine the above ingredients in a small blender or bowl and mix thoroughly to create a dressing, then pour the dressing over the salad and combine evenly, before serving. Options to consider for this recipe include adding other items you may have in your refrigerator:

- Cooked chicken breast, salmon, or turkey
- Roasted almonds, pumpkin seeds, and other seeds or nuts
- Fresh or dried mango, peach, or pineapple pieces

Spinach and Cranberry Salad

Preparation time: 20 minutes

Makes 2-4 servings

This salad is a variation on the kale salad, which contains dried fruits and goat cheese. This recipe includes orange zest and juice for a fruity flavor, which complements the bitterness of spinach.

- 1 bunch of fresh spinach, stems removed, sliced and washed
- ½ cups of goat cheese
- ½ cups of dried cranberries
- ¼ cups of thinly sliced red onion
- 3 tablespoons of dry toasted sliced almonds

Combine the spinach and goat cheese, then stir in the onion and set aside. In a separate bowl, combine the following ingredients to make the dressing:

- ½ cups of balsamic vinegar dressing
- 2 tablespoons of orange zest
- 2 tablespoons of orange juice, freshly squeezed

Mix the salad dressing ingredients until evenly combined, then pour over the spinach salad, and top with cranberries and almonds. Other options for toppings include walnut and pecans, which can be added in place of the almonds or with them.

Arugula and Kale Caesar Salad

Preparation time: 45 minutes

Makes 2-4 servings

This is a twist on the common lettuce-based Caesar salad, which often contains only a few ingredients, including croutons, bacon bits, and dressing. This variation combines arugula with kale to provide a stronger, more robust texture and flavor. This recipe remains simple, with the option of including croutons or substituting with baked chickpeas as an added protein instead.

- 1 small bunch of kale (any variety)
- ½ bunch of arugula (or less)
- 1/3 cups of grated parmesan cheese
- 1/3 cups of mayonnaise (low-fat is an option)
- 2 tablespoons skim milk
- 1 tablespoon of fresh lemon juice
- 1 tablespoon of Dijon mustard
- 2 crushed garlic cloves
- Dash of black pepper
- Dash of chili or cayenne pepper

- ½ cup of roasted chickpeas (oven-roasted for 20 minutes, coated in olive oil on 350 degrees)

Combine the cheese, mayonnaise, milk, lemon juice, mustard, cloves, and peppers in a medium bowl to make the dressing. Remove the stems from the kale and slice the leaves into small, bite sizes. Slice the arugula into small sizes, and toss both kale and arugula into a large bowl. Carefully pour the salad dressing into the bowl and coat evenly. Coat with extra parmesan cheese and roasted chickpeas, then serve.

Snacks and Sides for Any Time of the Day (and On the Go)

If you live a busy lifestyle, eating on-the-go is a constant reality that you may have difficulty escaping from, and home-cooked meals are far and few in between. For people living fast-paced, there are some quick and easy recipe options, as well as easy food combinations and selections that are recommended to keep you healthy and full of energy on the go. Often, it may be tempting to grab a bag of chips or a chocolate bar, both of which cause inflammation among other health conditions. When there are healthy snack options available, they tend to be expensive and not always the best options either, because of preservatives or the impact it has on the budget.

Kale Chips

Preparation time: 15 minutes

Cooking time: 8-10 minutes

Makes 5-6 servings

If you plan on using kale regularly, you may want to try making kale chips. There are a few variations with simple ingredients, depending on whether you prefer low sodium or plant-based options. This recipe is easy to prepare and often work best with kale with a smoother texture.

- 1 bunch of kale, stems removed and leaves sliced into small pieces
- Sea salt
- Olive oil

Prepare and slice the kale and preheat the oven to 350 degrees. Lightly coat each piece of kale with olive oil and sprinkle with salt, ensuring all kale is covered evenly. Bake in the oven for approximately 10 minutes. Keep an eye on the kale, as it can easily overcook, even within an extra minute, or remain slightly raw. When the chips are ready, they should be light and crispy and ready to enjoy.

Other options for coating and flavoring kale chips include powdered parmesan for a cheesy taste and to avoid using salt and reduce sodium. Chili pepper is another option, as well as cumin and/or cayenne pepper.

Trail Mix Recipe 1

Preparation time: 15 minutes

Makes 1-2 servings

An easy mix to create from nuts and seeds, trail mixes are often found packaged in natural food stores or in the bulk section of your local grocery store. Creating your own combination of nuts, seeds, and dried fruits is an ideal way to customize your snacks and avoid the temptation of sugary and salty options you may encounter. The nutritious content of your trail mix depends on the variety of options you choose.

- 1 cup of raw cashews
- 1 cup of sliced, dry roasted almonds
- 1 cup of pumpkin seeds
- 1 cup of dried, coconut flakes
- ½ cup of dark chocolate chips

- 2 teaspoons of cinnamon

Combine the ingredients together in a large or medium bowl and test taste. Add more ingredients as needed. Divide into 4 portions and seal in reusable bags for snacks on the go.

Trail Mix Recipe 2

Preparation time: 15 minutes

Makes 2-3 servings

This recipe offers a more "salty" or savory flavor combination:

- 1 cup of crushed peanuts
- 2 teaspoons sea salt
- ½ cups of pistachios shelled
- ½ cups of dried cranberries
- ½ cups of chia seeds
- ½ cups of sunflower seeds

Ensure all the seeds and nuts in this mix are unsalted, as a small amount of salt will be added to the mix. Increase portion size as desired, either by adding more of certain items or a little of each altogether. Divide into small portions of 3-4 and seal for snacks on the go.

Customize Your Trail Mix

Choosing the right ingredients to customize your trail mix will get easier and fun, as you discover more options to try. In addition to nuts and seeds, consider the number of dried fruits, chocolate, and yogurt-covered treats available in your local bulk store. Building your own mix is less expensive and will improve over time, as you become accustomed to the variety of options available:

- Cashews, peanuts, pistachios, almonds, pecans, walnuts, macadamia nuts
- Chia seeds, pumpkin, hemp, flax, sunflower, and sesame seeds
- Dried fruits: cherries, raisins, coconut flakes, berries, mango, peach, dates
- Dark chocolate chips, pretzel pieces, yogurt covered fruits, nuts, or chocolates

In addition to these options, you'll find many other ingredients to experiment with and add each time you create your trail mix. Avoid using salted and sweetened options as much as possible, or limit their use, so that your mix is healthy and promotes anti-inflammatory properties as much as possible.

Baked Squash

An easy, yet satisfying dish to prepare, is roasting squash in the oven for approximately 45 minutes to one hour. Squash is a nutrient-rich vegetable that contains a lot of vitamins C, A, and B6. It contains a lot of fiber, potassium, phosphorus, and magnesium. Consuming squash regularly can contribute to improving your body's ability to break down carbohydrates and fats, as well as strengthing bones and muscles. It is also an excellent anti-inflammatory and provides relief from the pain and discomfort of inflammation.

Oven-roasted squash is delicious and can be easily done with a baking pot, olive oil, and any variety of squash. Preheat the oven to 350 degrees and poke holes in the squash with a fork, then bake, unsliced, for approximately 45 minutes. This will soften the interior of the squash, and make it easier to chop in half and cook more. Remove from the oven and slice lengthwise, then coat the flesh or interior side lightly with olive oil, and cook faced down on a parchment paper-lined sheet, for another 20-30 minutes until done. Serve on its own with butter and/or black pepper as a side dish or light meal on its own.

Varieties of Squash

There are many types of squash available in different regions, and depending on where you live, you may find several varieties at your local grocery store. The following types are most common and often used in a variety of recipes:

- Butternut squash is long and light orange or beige in color. This variety of squash if most popular in soups, such as butternut squash soup, sometimes made with curry and/or coconut milk.
- Carnival squash is round and often colorful, ranging from dark green to light orange as it ripens. It's shaped like a small pumpkin and tends to have a sweeter flavor than other varieties, and excellent for roasting or stewing for soup.
- Acorn squash has a similar size to carnival squash, only it remains dark green as it ripens with some orange color. This variety contains a more savory taste and makes a great baked dish or addition to any meal as a side serving.
- Spaghetti squash is unique for its noodle-like flesh, and it often used as a substitute for spaghetti in some pasta dishes to replace regular noodles. The outside of this vegetable is light

yellow and long, similar to the size of butternut squash, only brighter in color.

There are many other types of squash available throughout the year and more so during the fall season. They tend to keep long outside of the refrigerator, though should be used quickly once sliced and cooked.

Butternut Squash Soup

Preparation time: 30 minutes

Cooking time: 1 hour, 30 minutes

Makes 6-8 servings

This is a creamy, tasty soup that can serve as a meal on its own or as an appetizer. The recipe includes butternut squash, though any variety can be used if available. The ingredients are easy to find and everything can be prepared in a single cooking pot.

- 1 tablespoon of olive oil
- 3 cloves of garlic (crushed)
- 1 medium onion, chopped in small pieces
- 1 teaspoon of sea salt
- 1 teaspoon of black pepper
- 1 teaspoon of thyme (dried)

- 1 medium or large butternut squash, roasted and sliced in half, lengthwise
- 1 cup of coconut milk
- 4 cups of vegetable or chicken stock

Prepare the squash once by the baking whole for 45 minutes, then slicing in half and removing the pits. Remove the flesh and chop into small, bite-sized cubes and set aside. Add olive oil to the bottom of a large cooking pot on the stovetop on medium heat, then add onion, garlic, pepper, thyme, and salt. Sauté the mixture until softened, then add in the soup stock and continue to cook and medium heat, adding in the squash and cooking for about 30 minutes. Remove the pot from the stove and cool slightly, then stir in the coconut milk. Using a large food processor or blender, blend the soup in batches, making sure there are no lumps remaining and that all ingredients are smooth and even throughout the soup. After each batch is blended, return to the cooking pot and continue to stew for another 20-30 minutes, then remove from heat and serve.

There are a few variations to consider for this recipe that you may want to try:

- Add one carrot to the squash while cooking
- Add one small yam or sweet potato

- A dash of dried ginger
- 2-3 tablespoons of curry powder, adding a bit of coconut curry to the base

Spaghetti Squash Pasta

Preparation time: 30 minutes

Cooking time: 1 hour, 30 minutes

Makes 4-6 servings

If you are looking to replace traditional pasta noodles with a healthier, more nutrient-packed vegetable, this dish is an excellent option. Spaghetti squash provides the noodle-like flesh inside that can serve as the "spaghetti," hence its name. It can be roasted whole in the oven to prepare and sliced lengthwise. The squash exterior itself can provide the bowl in which the "spaghetti" and other ingredients are served, once the pits or seeds are removed.

- ½ pound of lean ground beef
- 1 can of tomato sauce
- ¼ cups of parmesan cheese
- 1 green pepper (sliced into small pieces, length and width wise)
- ½ cup of sliced mushrooms
- 1 small onion

- 2-3 garlic cloves, crushed

  2 teaspoons of oregano
- 1 tablespoon of dried parsley
- Sea salt and black pepper to taste

In a medium saucepan, add the olive oil and simmer, adding the ground beef and cook until tender and brown. Add in the onions, garlic, and green peppers, then add in the spices and continue to cook. Add the mushrooms and tomato sauce, reduce heat, and continue to cook for another 20 minutes, then remove from heat. To prepare the squash, bake for 45 minutes, then slice lengthwise and remove seeds inside. Gently "scoop" the noodly flesh, on both pieces of the squash, so that it becomes easy to lift and eat. Pour the pasta sauce containing the ground beef over both squash halves and top with parmesan cheese before serving.

If you're vegan, substitute the ground beef for a vegan meat alternative, or add in more vegetables to the sauce while it's prepared, such as spinach, zucchini, and celery. Ensure all ingredients are cooked well and softened before pouring into the squash. Parmesan cheese topping can be replaced with vegan soy or vegetable-based cheese.

While this dish takes time to prepare, it can be stored for 3 days in the refrigerator and be enjoyed at any time, without any further preparation, simply by reheating.

Cheese, Olive, and Vegetable Platter

Preparation time: 30 minutes

Makes 4-6 servings

This is a fun dish to prepare and can be sized according to one person, a small group, or a larger group of people. To avoid high sodium normally contained in cheese, choose low sodium varieties such as cream cheese, cottage cheese (including low-fat), mozzarella, Emmental, parmesan, ricotta, and Monterey Jack. If you prefer cheddar or another type of cheese that tends to contain more sodium, reduce the portion size. Olives are naturally anti-inflammatory and make a great addition to soups, sandwiches, and platters. Both black and green olives can be added; while green olives tend to be more sour to taste, black olives are slightly sweeter. Other items for the vegetable platter include raw vegetables, nuts, and seeds to create a complete meal that can provide all the nutrients you require in just one serving.

- 8-10 cherry tomatoes, sliced in half
- ½ cups of almonds

- ½ cups of cashews
- 1 cup of black or green olives, sliced or whole, and pitted
- 1 cup of cubed mozzarella cheese
- 2 cups of another cheese, such as Monterey Jack, parmesan or Emmental.
- 1-2 tablespoons of cottage cheese, on the side of the platter
- 3-4 celery stalks, sliced lengthwise
- 3-4 large carrots, peeled and sliced lengthwise

Arrange all ingredients in a large, oval platter and serve. Further items that can be added include baked salmon and/or smoked salmon rolled with cream cheese filling and capers. While smoked meat is high in sodium, a small portion of smoked salmon can be added on occasion if preferred. Adding pumpkin and sunflower seeds is another option, along with any other bite-sized savory foods available.

Chapter 6: Plant-based Anti-Inflammatory Foods

Eating Vegan and Anti-inflammatory: The Benefits of Combining Both

While it is not necessary to become vegan to reap the rewards of the anti-inflammatory diet, it can be extremely beneficial if you decide to work towards plant-based eating as a lifestyle choice. For many people, going vegan is an ethical decision, and it can provide a number of benefits, including the reduction and prevention of many diseases. There are many benefits to eating a plant-based diet, including:

- Focusing on eating more vegetables and fruits, all of which are high in nutrients
- Prevention of certain cancers. Some studies done on vegan diets indicate fewer incidents of cancer and overall better immune system function
- Improvements in heart health and less risk for heart disease
- Better kidney function and detoxification

- Reduction of symptoms associated with arthritis, including less pain, due to lower incidents of inflammation.
- Promotes weight loss and better metabolic function

Are there drawbacks to eating a plant-based diet? Aside from making sure you get all of your nutrients and taking extra time to choose your foods carefully for their vitamins, minerals, and protein content, there are no ill effects of a vegan diet. Most people feel more energized and able to become more active. Plant-based foods promote faster digestion, which can improve gut health.

Plant-based Recipes and Food Ideas

Vegan meal planning may take a while if you're new to a plant-based diet, though overall, it can simplify how you arrange your meals and get your nutrients. The following recipes are easy and require only a handful of ingredients. Before you begin, you may want to become familiar with soy-based foods, which are a staple in the vegan diet:

- Tofu is a common food item in vegan diets and can be purchased firm (for stir fry and skillet dishes) or soft (for puddings and cream sauces).

- Tempeh is fermented soy and often available where tofu is found in most grocery stores and natural food stores. It is firm in texture and can be roasted or marinated much like regular meats.
- Miso is a fermented soy-based paste used in making sauces, soups, or marinades.
- Soy-based meats and cheeses vary in quality and taste. Be cautious when choosing from these products, as they may contain preservatives found in some of their non-vegan versions, such as carcinogens and nitrates. Smoked tofu, for example, is a tasty treat that many vegans enjoy, though it may contain preservatives that should be avoided on a regular basis.

Tofu Scramble

Preparation time: 30 minutes (soak tofu overnight or for a minimum of 2 hours)

Cooking time: 10 minutes

Makes 1-2 servings

This is a simple vegan version of the popular scrambled eggs dish. It takes a bit of preparation, though it's easy to cook once ready. Tofu takes on the flavor of another ingredient, like a sponge, which makes it an ideal food for marinating. To strengthen or infuse flavor into tofu, marinating or soaking tofu in a variety of sauces, broths, or juices is ideal in preparation for many dishes. For this breakfast, one block of tofu is marinated in a sealed container of vegetable broth (either store-bought or prepared from scratch). Species such as black pepper, sea salt, and turmeric are added to further enhance the flavor, and other ingredients can be added:

- 1 block of firm tofu
- 1 carton or 2 cups of vegetarian broth
- 2 teaspoons of miso paste (white or yellow miso paste)
- 2 tablespoons ground turmeric
- 1 teaspoon black pepper
- 1 teaspoon of sea salt

Place the block of tofu into a medium container (chop into several pieces, if desired). In a small or medium bowl, combine the vegetable broth with spices and stir. Pour vegetable broth over to coat the entire block of tofu and refrigerate overnight, or for at least two hours. When ready to use, heat a skillet on medium heat with olive oil. Drain the tofu and retain ¼ cup of liquid. Mash the tofu in a separate bowl and add more spices, if desired. Add to the skillet and fry, adding in the liquid and add any other ingredients you normally would with scrambled eggs, including:

- Chopped onions
- Spinach
- Sliced green peppers
- Sliced mushrooms

Serve with toast or with sliced avocado.

Avocado Toast

Preparation time: 10 minutes

Makes 1-2 servings

A tasty open-faced sandwich, avocado toast can be enjoyed at any time of day. Choose a hearty bread with lots of seeds and/or a rye or flaxseed bread. Toast and butter with vegan butter or lightly drizzle olive oil, then add sliced avocado. Avocados should be ripe enough to slice, though not overripe to mash. If the avocado is overripe, it can be mashed and spread on the toast instead. Sprinkle with black pepper and toasted sesame seeds to enjoy:

- 1 large avocado
- 2 slices of bread, toasted
- Lightly dry roasted sesame seeds

- Black pepper to taste

Tempeh Skillet Plate

Preparation time: 30 minutes

Cooking time: 15-30 minutes

Makes 3-4 servings

Tempeh is prepared and cooked like beef and other textured types of meat. The best way to prepare this food is by marinating in the following:

- 1 block of tempeh, sliced into bite-size cubes
- 1-2 cups of vegetarian broth
- ½ cup low sodium soy sauce
- 2 crushed garlic cloves
- 1 chopped onion
- 1 teaspoon of black pepper

Combine all ingredients above and pour over the tempeh cubes in a sealable container. Refrigerate for two hours, then prepare a skillet with olive oil and add the tempeh. Sauté on medium for 10-15 minutes, then reduce heat and add the following ingredients:

- 2 chopped celery stalks
- 2 carrots, chopped in small pieces

- 2 crushed garlic cloves
- 1 cup of snow peas
- ½ cup of basil leaves
- ½ green pepper, sliced
- ½ red pepper, sliced

Continue to sauté and mix the vegetables, until they are all cooked, then add the following:

- ¼ cup sliced mushrooms
- 1 cup of bean sprouts

Once all the ingredients are cooked, serve on rice or on a plate with a side salad or soup.

Guacamole

Preparation time: 20 minutes

Makes 2-4 servings

A simple avocado-based dip, guacamole can be served on bread, in tacos, or as a dip for chips. This recipe adds a few salsa ingredients for some spice:

- 2 ripe avocados, pitted, peeled, and mashed.
- Juice of 2 limes
- 2 tablespoons olive oil
- 1 tablespoon chili powder
- 1 jalapeno pepper, sliced thinly

- Sea salt and black pepper to taste
- ½ cup chopped cilantro or parsley
- 1 small onion, chopped
- 1 small tomato, chopped

Mash both avocados in a medium bowl, and add all of the ingredients. Fold ingredients together until evenly mixed, then serve in a bowl as a dip, spread or side dish.

Potato and Lentil Patties

Preparation time: 20 minutes

Cooking time: 10-15 minutes

Makes 2-4 servings

- 1 cup of red lentils
- 2 cloves of crushed garlic
- 2 medium potatoes
- 1 small onion, chopped finely
- 1 carrot, chopped
- 5 tablespoons of flour
- 1 teaspoon of paprika
- 1 teaspoon of black pepper
- 1 teaspoon of dried dill (optional)
- 1 teaspoon of marjoram

Cook the lentils in a saucepan. Cover and reduce heat while preparing the potatoes. Grate the potatoes and carrot together and add to a medium bowl. Drain and add the lentils, then add the garlic, onion, flour, and spices. Combine and form into balls to make patties. Heat a skillet on medium with olive oil, and fry each patty for approximately 4 minutes on each side. As an alternative, bake the patties all at once in the oven for 20 minutes on 350 degrees. Serve with vegan sour cream or hot sauce.

Sautéed Asparagus with Almonds

Preparation time: 10 minutes

Cooking time (for spinach): 10-15 minutes

Makes 2-4 servings

An easy and delicious dish to prepare, this meal requires only three major ingredients and a skillet:

- 1 bunch of asparagus, cleaned and chopped into long 3-4 inch pieces
- ½ cup of toasted sliced almonds
- ½ cup of vegan parmesan cheese
- Dash of salt and black pepper

Heat a skillet on medium and add olive oil. Once the skillet is ready, add the asparagus and cook until tender. Add a bit of vegan shredded parmesan cheese. If the vegan cheese is soy-based, it will not melt, though vegetable-based vegan cheese does and might be a good option for this dish. Continue to sauté until asparagus is softened and ready to serve. Top with the remaining cheese and roasted almonds, then serve.

Lentil Daal

Preparation time: 45 minutes to one hour

Makes 2-4 servings

An easy, tasty side dish or main meal, lentil daal is popular in India and is enjoyed as a healthy, warm, comfort food. This recipe includes red lentils, which tend to cook quickly and absorb spices well.

- 1 cup of red lentils
- 1 tablespoon of olive oil
- 1 cinnamon stick (optional)
- 1 teaspoon cumin seeds
- 1 cup of diced onion
- 3-4 crushed garlic cloves
- 1 teaspoon minced ginger
- 1 teaspoon ground cardamom

- 1 teaspoon turmeric
- 1 teaspoon of paprika
- 1 medium tomato, chopped
- Dash of sea salt
- 2 green chilis, seeded, stems removed and chopped finely

Rinse the lentils and add to a large saucepan with three cups of water. Cook for 30 minutes. While the lentils cook, prepare a skillet with olive oil and add the cumin seeds and cinnamon stick and cook for about two minutes. Add the onion, garlic, chili peppers, ginger, and pepper and cook for another 5-6 minutes. Add the turmeric, cardamom, paprika, and salt, along with the diced tomato and continue to cook. Reduce heat, and wait until the lentils are fully cooked, then add them to the skillet and mix, continuing to cook on low-medium heat. Remove and serve with cilantro.

Hummus Dip

Preparation time: 20 minutes

Makes 2-4 servings

One way to enjoy vegan cuisine is through creamy dips and sauces full of flavor and spice. Hummus is created with chickpeas, tahini (sesame butter), olive oil, lemon, and cumin.

- 1 can of chickpeas
- 1/3 cups of freshly squeezed lemon juice
- ¼ cups of tahini (at room temperature)
- 2-3 tablespoons of water
- 1 teaspoon of paprika
- 1 teaspoon of cumin
- 2-3 tablespoons of olive oil
- 1-2 garlic cloves, crushed

Combine all ingredients in a food processor and blend until equally blended, ensuring there are no lumps. Ensure the canned chickpeas are drained and thoroughly rinsed before adding to the food processor. Add a teaspoon of chili pepper or crushed jalapeno peppers for a bit of heat. These can be added as a topping or combined in the food processor.

Hummus and Lentil Dip

Preparation time: 20 minutes

Makes 2-4 servings

If you have a handful of leftover lentils from daal or a previous meal, this is a great way to use them! Add ½ cup of red lentils as part of the following ingredients:

- 1 can of chickpeas
- ½ cup of cooked red lentils
- 1/3 cups of freshly squeezed lemon juice
- ¼ cups of tahini (at room temperature)
- 2-3 tablespoons of water
- 1 teaspoon of turmeric
- 1 teaspoon of paprika
- 1 teaspoon of cumin
- 2-3 tablespoons of olive oil
- 1-2 garlic cloves, crushed

Add all ingredients into a food processor. Before adding the chickpeas and lentils, drain and rinse. If the lentils were previously cooked and are coated in sauce, this can either be added into the recipe, or they can be drained and added to the processor.

Hummus Beetroot Dip

Preparation time: 45 minutes

Cooking time (for beetroot): 10-15 minutes

Makes 2-4 servings

Beets are rich in iron and fiber and provide a new flavor to a traditional hummus dip. To prepare beets, they can either be juiced raw or lightly stewed, so they become soft and milder in flavor. If this is your first time adding beetroot to a dish, especially a dip, try one small beet, cut into quarters, and steam on the stovetop. Bring to a boil, then reduce heat to low and cook for another 15-20 minutes. Drain the beets and set aside to add to the following recipe:

- 1 can of chickpeas
- 1 small beetroot (steamed or raw, chopped in small pieces)
- 1/3 cups of freshly squeezed lemon juice
- ¼ cups of tahini (at room temperature)
- 2-3 tablespoons of water
- 1 teaspoon of dried parsley
- 1 teaspoon of paprika
- 1 teaspoon of cumin
- 2-3 tablespoons of olive oil
- 1-2 garlic cloves, crushed

Combine all ingredients, including the drained chickpeas and beetroot into the food processor. Blend well and serve. Parsley is included in this recipe to enhance the flavor of beets and chickpeas, though it can be used as a garnish instead.

Other options for hummus include the following:

- Substitute beetroot with roasted yams
- Create an eggplant dip by replacing the chickpeas in the basic hummus recipe with one oven-roasted eggplant.
- Add caramelized onions as a topping for regular hummus or blend into the recipe.
- Juice spinach and/or kale and add to the hummus ingredients before blending.

Spinach Hummus

Preparation time: 20 minutes

Cooking time (for spinach): 5-10 minutes

Makes 2-4 servings

- 1 can of red chickpeas (pre-cooked)
- 2-3 large cloves of garlic, crushed
- 2 teaspoons of cumin seeds
- 1 small onion, sliced

- 1 cup of frozen spinach
- 1 teaspoon of sea salt
- 1 tablespoon lemon juice
- 2 tablespoons olive oil
- ½ cups of tahini (sesame butter)

In a skillet on medium heat, add olive oil and sautee the onions for 5-6 minutes, until tender. Thaw the frozen spinach in the microwave and add to the onions, and cook for another 3-4 minutes. Remove from heat and cool for 10 minutes. In a food processor, combine the chickpeas, spinach, onions and tahini and pulse for 30-45 seconds. Add the lemon juice, olive oil, crushed garlic, cumin, and sea salt and continue to blend until smooth. Taste test and add 1-2 teaspoons of oil or water if needed.

Roasted Garlic Hummus

Preparation time: 20 minutes

Cooking time (for roasting garlic): 20-25 minutes

Makes 2-4 servings
- 1 can of red chickpeas (pre-cooked)
- 1 small garlic, roasted in the oven
- 2 cloves of garlic (raw), crushed

- 2 teaspoons of cumin seeds
- 1 small onion, sliced
- 1 teaspoon of sea salt
- 1 tablespoon lemon juice
- 2 tablespoons olive oil
- ½ cups of tahini (sesame butter)

Preheat the oven to 350 degrees and roast one whole garlic for 20-25 minutes, or until soft. Remove from heat and set aside. Remove from heat and cool for 10 minutes. In a food processor, combine the chickpeas, roasted garlic (peeled and softened), and tahini and pulse for 30-45 seconds. Add the lemon juice, olive oil, crushed garlic, cumin, and sea salt and continue to blend until smooth. Taste test and add 1-2 teaspoons of oil or water if needed.

Chapter 7: Meats, Poultry, and Seafood

Seafood Recipes

Fish is an excellent source of calcium, protein, and healthy fats and can be a great part of an anti-inflammatory diet. The best fish to choose is salmon, which is low in sodium and high in nutrients. Preparing salmon is best done on a grill or in the oven and can be seasoned according to personal preference, either spicy or savory, or both. Salmon tends to be mild in flavor, which makes it easy to combine with many other ingredients.

Baked Salmon in Garlic Sauce

Preparation time: 20 minutes

Cooking time: 45 minutes

Makes 1-2 servings

The salmon can be either fresh or frozen. If frozen, allow time to thaw before using in this recipe.

- 1 large salmon fillet, or two small fillets
- 2 lemons

- Dash of sea salt
- Dash of black pepper
- 1 teaspoon of oregano
- 1 teaspoon of thyme
- 1 teaspoon of honey or natural sweetener
- 4-6 tablespoons of softened butter
- Fresh parsley as a topping
- 2 cloves of garlic, crushed

Prepare the oven to 350 degrees and line a large baking dish with tin foil, then coat lightly in olive oil. Slice the two lemons in thin slices and arrange evenly over the foil. Take the salmon fillet and season both sides with spices and arrange on top of the lemon slices. Add butter, then wrap the salmon and bake for 30 minutes, then change to broil and continue cooking for another 2-3 minutes until done. Serve with parsley and additional lemon.

Tuna and Avocado Tacos

Preparation time: 25 minutes

Makes 2-4 servings

Tuna is an inexpensive and highly nutritious fish that can be adapted to many dishes. In this recipe, canned tuna is used and often most available and convenient to work with. This recipe is easy to prepare and requires the following ingredients:

- 1-2 cans tuna (flaky tuna in water, drained)
- ¼ cups of low-fat mayonnaise
- 1-2 teaspoons of freshly squeezed lemon juice
- ¼ cup of scallion
- 2 teaspoons of avocado oil
- 4 medium-sized tortillas
- 1-2 avocados, firm but ripe
- 2 tablespoons of freshly squeezed lime or lemon juice

Combine the mayonnaise, avocado oil, lime or lemon juice, and scallions in a small bowl then set aside. Heat a skillet and add a bit of avocado oil, and then add the tuna, Sauté for a few minutes until fish is browned, then remove from heat. Lightly grill each tortilla, then remove and fill with sliced avocado, tuna, and the creamy sauce. Garnish with dill and/or parsley.

For variations to this recipe, add chili pepper to enhance the spiciness. Turmeric powder can be added directly to the sauce or sprinkled on top before serving.

Tuna Patties

Preparation time: 20 minutes

Cooking time (for roasting garlic): 10-15 minutes

Makes 2-4 servings

If you are looking for an easy way to make dinner and feed a lot of people, tuna patties are a great option and take little time to prepare. While there are a lot of ingredients to include, the recipe is simple to follow and the preparation time is reasonable, making it an easy dish to pull together within a short period of time.

- 2 cans of tuna (flaky tuna in water, drained)
- ½ of bread crumbs
- 1 tablespoon of grated lemon zest
- 1 teaspoon of lemon juice
- 1 raw egg
- 2 tablespoons of olive oil
- ¼ tablespoon of soft butter
- 2 tablespoons of dried parsley
- 1-2 teaspoons of dried dill
- Ground black pepper (to taste)
- 1 teaspoon of tabasco sauce or a similar hot sauce
- 2 teaspoons of Dijon mustard
- 2 teaspoons of chives or sliced green onions

- 1 tablespoon of water (water from the tuna can be used)

Before you begin, make sure the canned tuna is thoroughly drained, and at least one or two tablespoons of the water is reserved. Add olive oil to the tuna and mix the following ingredients in a small bowl, along with the tuna and oil: mustard, lemon zest, bread crumbs, water, parsley, hot sauce, chives or green onions, salt, pepper, and egg. Mix well and form into patties. Heat a skillet on medium with olive oil, and gently arrange one or two patties on the skillet, frying each side for approximately 3 or 4 minutes. Both sides of the patty should brown slightly. Serve with a bun or on its own. To make tartar sauce, simply combine ¼ cup of mayonnaise with ¼ cup of green relish. Add a dollop of sauce to the top of the patty and enjoy it.

Tuna Melt Avocados

Preparation time: 30 minutes

Makes 2-4 servings

Tuna and avocados work well together due to their flavor combination and the high amount of protein, vitamins, calcium, and healthy fats they contain. This recipe is easy to create and can be made with just a handful of ingredients.

- 2 cans of tuna, drained
- ¼ cups of finely chopped bell pepper
- ¼ cup of sliced red onion (thin slices)
- ¼ cup of mayonnaise
- Dash of salt and pepper
- 3 avocadoes, cut in half and pits removed
- 2 tablespoons of chipotle hot sauce
- 2-3 teaspoons of cilantro

Combine the tuna, peppers, onion, and mayonnaise in a small or medium bowl and mix thoroughly. Add in the cilantro and continue to mix. Remove some of the flesh from each of the avocados and combine with the tuna, then fill each half with the hot sauce drizzled on top. Serve immediately.

Variations to this recipe include using canned salmon or chicken if the tuna is not available or preferred.

Poultry and Meat Recipes

Chicken and turkey are ideal for the anti-inflammatory diet and can be prepared in many ways. The best method of getting the most out of your poultry is by using the meat in its entirety, including the bones for broth. Roasting a chicken or turkey may seem like a lot of work initially, though it will cut down your efforts tremendously over the course of a week, and provide many meal options.

Oven Roast Chicken

Preparation time: 45 minutes

Cooking time: 2-3 hours

Makes 6-8 servings

Choosing a free-range, organic, and locally raised chicken is the best option. If you have enough room in your freezer, it may be advantageous to buy two or three to have on hand for future meals. Chicken is available throughout the year and can be found in all grocery stores, including farmers' markets and natural food stores (for natural, hormone-free varieties). When preparing the chicken, remove the giblets to make a gravy. Preheat the oven to 350 degrees and line a large baking pan with parchment paper, lightly coated in olive oil. Wash the chicken and place it inside the pan. In a small bowl, combine the following spices with 3-4 teaspoons of olive oil:

- 2 tablespoons of poultry seasoning
- 3 teaspoons of dried sage
- 3 teaspoons of thyme
- 2 teaspoons of dried basil (optional)
- 1 teaspoon of paprika
- Dash of sea salt and black pepper

In a small bowl, whisk together the spices and olive oil, then evenly coat the chicken before roasting. For more flavor options, coarsely chop two small onions into quarters (skins removed) and stuff inside the chicken. This can be done with garlic cloves as well. Bake in the oven for 2-3 hours, checking in every 45 minutes to baste. Re-coat the chicken and ensure that it is not drying. For best results, roast chicken in a large baking pot with a lid. Once the chicken is done, remove from the oven and serve with any side dishes or on its own. Good options for sides include mashed potatoes with garlic and gravy, lightly steamed vegetables, roasted yams and/or squash, and Brussels sprouts.

Remove any leftover chicken from the bones and store in the refrigerator for future use. The bones can be used to prepare a bone broth, as detailed earlier in this book.

Chicken Giblet Gravy

Preparation time: 10 minutes

Cooking time: 15 minutes

Makes 6-8 servings

This is an easy recipe that makes good use of the giblets inside the chicken (or turkey):

- 4 cups of water
- 1 cup of chicken drippings
- 1 full set of giblets from the chicken
- 5-6 tablespoons of cornstarch
- 1 cooked egg (optional)
- Dash of sea salt and black pepper

In a large saucepan, pour the four cups of water over the giblets and boil, then reduce the heat to low. Drain the water and combine ¼ of the giblets and drippings in a small saucepan. Heat on medium and add cornstarch and an additional cup of water, plus the broth prepared from the giblets. Add the cooked egg to the blend, then the salt and pepper. Continue to simmer until thick enough to serve as gravy.

Oven Roast Turkey

Preparation time: 45 minutes

Cooking time: 3-4 hours

Makes 6-8 servings

Like chicken, turkey is prepared in the same fashion, though it may take longer to roast due to the size, closer to 3-4 hours. Ingredients, seasoning, and preparation can be done in the same way as chicken, only there are some key options you may want to consider the following:

- Turkey giblet gravy (prepared the same as for chicken)
- Cranberry sauce
- Stuffing options

Cranberry Sauce

Preparation time: 15 minutes

Cooking time: 20-30 minutes

Makes 6-8 servings

The canned variety of cranberry sauce is high in sugar, though it can be easily prepared from fresh cranberries, usually available in most grocery stores. Frozen cranberries are also available as an option when fresh is unavailable.

- 2 cups of fresh or frozen (thawed) cranberries
- 1 large orange (all the juice and zest)
- 1 small apple, sliced into small cubes
- ¼ cup of natural or low carb sweetener
- 3-4 cups of water

In a small saucepan, combine the water with the cranberries and bring to a boil. Maintain the boiling for 10 minutes and keep the berries covered with a lid. Remove from the stove and drain some of the water, retaining enough to coat the cranberries, which should be reduced in size. Add the orange juice, zest, apple, and sweetener and continue to stew on low-medium heat for another 30 minutes. Remove from heat and cool at room temperature, then transfer to a glass bowl or jar and refrigerate until ready for use. Cranberry sauce can be stored for a week or more in the fridge or frozen for later use.

Stir-Fried Chicken or Beef

Preparation time: 45 minutes

Cooking time: 30 minutes

Makes 6-8 servings

One of the most versatile and easy dishes to make is a stir fry, otherwise known as a skillet dish. Chicken or beef can be used with any variety of vegetables. Olive oil is the best option for cooking. To reduce sodium and inflammation-causing foods, avoid adding too many condiments or soy sauce. If desired, use a sodium-reduced soy sauce for stir fry dishes or a teriyaki sauce.

If you have leftover beef, chicken, or turkey from a roast dinner, these can be used as part of the skillet dish and will generally take less time to cook. Vegetables to consider for inclusion in this recipe:

- Snow peas
- Watercress (sliced in small, round disks)
- Carrots
- Celery
- Bean sprouts
- Mushrooms
- Baby corn
- Basil leaves (fresh)

Heat a skillet on medium and add olive oil, then add the chicken or beef. If the meat is raw, cook thoroughly before adding any other ingredients. Add soy sauce while cooking the meat, if desired, or sodium-reduced teriyaki. Once the meat is cooked, add carrots, celery, snow peas, baby corn, and other vegetables that take longer to fry. Once these items are cooked, add mushrooms, basil leaves, and bean sprouts. Serve on rice or on its own in a bowl.

Skillet Breakfast

If you have leftover stir fry from a previous lunch or dinner, consider adding it to the skillet for breakfast the next morning with a serving of scrambled eggs. If you follow a plant-based diet, firm tofu marinated in vegetable broth can be used, and meat omitted from the stir fry for a vegan meal. The scrambled tofu recipe is detailed in the plant-based recipe section and can be prepared as easy as the egg version.

To prepare a skillet breakfast, heat a frying pan with olive oil and add crushed garlic and black pepper. In a small bowl, whisk two or three eggs and add to the skillet and cook until nearly done, then add any of the leftover items from the stir fry and continue on medium heat until ready. Serve on its own or with toast. Options for this dish include adding chili pepper and/or paprika to the eggs for spice. If there are only select ingredients from the stir fry you prefer to add, just omit the rest and use them in another dish, or simply enjoy as leftovers on their own.

Turkey Rice Egg Drop Soup

Preparation time: 15-20 minutes

Cooking time: 30 minutes

Makes 6-8 servings

An ideal soup made from a festive turkey dinner, this dish can be made using turkey bone broth (prepared like chicken or beef broth) and any leftover vegetables, such as turkey meat, carrots, celery, peppers, and additional vegetables that you may find in your refrigerator. Bring the broth to a boil, with the turkey and leftovers, then add 1-2 cups of basmati or jasmine rice (any variety of rice can be used, if neither are available). As the rice cooks, keep the heat on medium and continue to stir, adding more water or broth if needed. In a small bowl, add two eggs and whisk together, then add to the soup, and continue to stir until the rice and eggs are fully cooked, then serve.

Other ingredients that can enhance the flavor of this soup include the following:

- Basil leaves (dried or fresh)
- Bay leaves
- 1 tablespoon of soy sauce (low sodium)

Chapter 8: Desserts

Cakes and Pie Recipes

Avoiding sugar and processed foods often means skipping desserts, though this doesn't have to be an option with a healthier version of a recipe. Some of the most decadent cakes and pies can be easily translated into recipes that contain lower calories and reduced sugar for a guilt-free option.

Chocolate Cake

Preparation time: 30 minutes

Cooking time: 45 minutes

Makes 6-8 servings

This cake contains natural ingredients low in carbohydrates, which helps reduce instances of inflammation. Avoiding wheat flour and sugar are two major items that cause health conditions to flare up, including increasing blood sugar, cholesterol, and conditions that contribute to inflammation. Dark, unsweetened chocolate is the best option, as it contains antioxidants. Cocoa powder or baker's chocolate can be used for this recipe.

- 1 cup of coconut flour
- ¾ cups of low carb sweetener
- 1 cup of unsweetened cocoa powder, or the same portion in melted baker's chocolate (dark, unsweetened)
- 2 teaspoons of baking powder
- 2 teaspoons of baking soda
- 1 teaspoon of cinnamon
- Dash of sea salt
- 2 teaspoons of vanilla
- 4 cups of shredded zucchini
- ½ cup of melted coconut oil
- 8 eggs

Combine the cocoa or baker's chocolate, low carb sweetener, coconut flour, cinnamon, baking soda, baking powder, and sea salt and mix together well. If the melted baker's chocolate is chosen instead of the cocoa powder, mix the dry ingredients first, then add the baker's chocolate. Add eggs, coconut oil, and vanilla next and combine well, then stir in the shredded zucchini. If preferred, add chocolate chips or any additional chocolate ingredients you wish to add. Prepare the oven by preheating to 350 degrees and prepare a baking dish with parchment paper. Pour the mixture into the pan and bake for 40 minutes. Check with a toothpick once the cake is done to make sure it is baked thoroughly. Cool slightly, then slice and serve with coconut whipping cream. This cake can be refrigerated for up to one week.

Pumpkin Cake

Preparation time: 25 minutes

Cooking time: 35 minutes

Makes 6-8 servings

This is a tasty and healthy cake that can serve as a dessert or a quick breakfast. A muffin tin can be used to create muffins out of this recipe as an alternative.

- 2 cups of almond flour
- 1 teaspoon of baking soda
- 2 teaspoons of baking powder
- 1 teaspoon of sea salt
- 2 teaspoons of cinnamon
- 2 teaspoons of pumpkin spice, or combine ½ teaspoon cloves, 1 teaspoon cinnamon, and 1 teaspoon nutmeg together
- 4 eggs
- 2 teaspoons of vanilla extract

- ½ cup low carb sweetener

Prepare the oven by preheating to 350 degrees. In two separate bowls, combine all wet ingredients in one and all the dry in the other. Once each bowl is thoroughly mixed, combine together and blend well. Prepare a baking dish with parchment paper and pour the mixture evenly. Bake for 30-35 minutes and test with a toothpick to confirm when it's ready. Sprinkle lightly with cinnamon or nutmeg on the top of the cake, and cool slightly before serving, or refrigerate and serve later.

Pie Shell Preparation

Preparation time: 15 minutes

Cooking time: 15 minutes

There is an easy way to create pie shells with just a few ingredients:

- Almond flour
- Coconut flour
- Coconut oil (melted)
- Low carb sweetener

The portions may vary depending on the size of the pie shell and how much you prefer to use coconut flour and almond flour. If only one of the two flours is used, add almond flour, as it is easier to work with. Coconut flour tends to dry fast, though it has a pleasant flavor that combines well with most baking ingredients. Use equal parts of coconut and almond flour for the best results. In a bowl, combine the following ingredients, adding more if needed:

- ½ cups of almond flour
- ½ cups of coconut flour
- 2 teaspoons low carb sweetener
- ¼ cups of coconut oil

Combine the ingredients in a small or medium bowl until evenly mixed, then spread on a pie tin, coating the bottom and sides consistently without any lumps. Bake in the oven for 10-15 minutes at 350 degrees or until lightly browned, then remove and set aside. This pie shell is ideal for many varieties of simple pie recipes.

Rhubarb and Strawberry Pie

Preparation time: 15-25 minutes

Cooking time: 45 minutes

Makes 6-8 servings

This is an easy pie to enjoy while rhubarb is in season. Strawberries are added to complement the sweet and sour combination taste.

- 3 cups of rhubarb, chopped into small pieces
- 1 cup of chopped strawberries (stems removed)
- 1 cup low carb sweetener
- 6 tablespoons of coconut flour
- 1 tablespoon butter

Combine the rhubarb and strawberries with the flour and sweetener, then add butter and mix thoroughly. Scoop into the pie shell and bake for 45 minutes at 400 degrees, then remove from heat and cool slightly before slicing and serving. This pie can be served either warm or cold. If desired, omit strawberries altogether and use four cups of rhubarb instead.

Blueberry and Blackberry Pie

Preparation time: 15-25 minutes

Cooking time: 45 minutes

Makes 6-8 servings

Like the rhubarb pie, blueberries and blackberries offer a different sweet and sour combination for a delicious result. Fresh berries are recommended, though frozen berries is an option, as long as they are thawed prior to this recipe:

- 3 cups of blackberries

- 2 cups of blueberries
- 1 cup low carb sweetener
- 1 teaspoon lemon juice
- 1 teaspoon lemon zest
- 1 teaspoon cinnamon (ground)
- ½ teaspoon almond extract

Combine all the ingredients in a large bowl, tossing until they are evenly mixed. Transfer them to a pie shell and bake for 30 minutes on 400 degrees.

Lime Cheesecake

Preparation time: 15-25 minutes

Cooking time: 50 minutes to one hour

Makes 6-8 servings

This cheesecake works well with the simple pie shell option. The ingredients include low carb sweetener to reduce the carbohydrates in this recipe:

- 1 package of cream cheese (low fat is an option)
- 4 eggs
- 2/3 cups of low-fat sour cream
- 1/3 cups of coconut cream
- 2 teaspoons of vanilla extract
- ½ cups of lime juice (or freshly squeezed)

- 1 cup of low carb sweetener (granulated)
- 1 tablespoon cornstarch

In a medium or large bowl, combine sugar and cornstarch and blend with an electric mixer until smooth. Before adding the cream cheese, ensure it softened at room temperature and mix, then add the eggs, followed by the lime juice and vanilla. Pour into the pie shell and bake for about 50 minutes. Cool before serving.

Other variations of this recipe include:

- Replacing lime with lemon or combining both for one pie
- Adding any variety of berries and blending with the filling
- Adding coconut flakes
- Melted dark chocolate and/or cocoa powder for a chocolate cheesecake

Puddings, Custards, and Ice Cream Desserts

Many of the simpler desserts available can be adapted to an anti-inflammatory diet and fit as part of a healthy lifestyle.

Avocado Chocolate Mousse

Preparation time: 5 minutes

Makes 1-2 servings

A healthy and quickly made dessert, this mousse combines three ingredients and takes a mere five minutes to prepare:

- 1 ripe avocado
- 2 tablespoons cocoa powder (unsweetened)
- 2-3 teaspoons of low carb sweeter, or honey or maple syrup

In a small bowl, add the ripe flesh of one avocado and mash. Add in the cocoa powder and sweetener, continuing to mash until mixed and ready to enjoy.

Chia Seed Pudding

Preparation time: 10 minutes (refrigerate overnight or for 2 hours)

Makes 1-2 servings

A simple, yet effective way to get all or most of your nutrients and enjoy a dessert-like treat, chia seed pudding is an excellent option for breakfast, as well as dessert. It provides a good boost of energy to begin the day and before heading to the gym. Chia seeds contain a good source of protein, calcium, fiber, antioxidants, fatty acids, and iron. They are often available in bulk stores and both natural food stores and grocers. For best quality, choose organic chia seeds. There are several varieties available, including black and reddish-brown seeds, though they all contain a comparable high nutrient value, earning them the "superfood" label.

Preparing chia seed pudding is as easy as combining ingredients and refrigerating overnight for best results. The following recipe is a basic version to start and can be modified to include a variety of flavors and additional ingredients:

- 1 cup of chia seeds
- 1 cup of coconut milk
- ½ cups cream (unsweetened) or coconut cream

- ¼ cups of low carb sweetener
- 1-2 teaspoons of vanilla

Combine the milk and cream in a medium bowl and whisk in the sweetener and chia seeds, followed by the vanilla. Once all ingredients are combined, transfer to a sealable container and refrigerate overnight. Serve in the morning or as a dessert topped with fresh fruit or crushed almonds, pistachios, or walnuts. Sprinkle with cinnamon for a "rice pudding" flavor.

Chocolate Chia Seed Pudding

Preparation time: 10 minutes (refrigerate overnight or for 2 hours)

Makes 1-2 servings

Chocolate chia pudding includes a dose of cocoa powder or melted baker's chocolate, in addition to the basic ingredients:

- 1 cup of chia seeds
- 1 cup of coconut milk
- ½ cups cream (unsweetened) or coconut cream
- ½ cup of cocoa powder (unsweetened)
- ¼ cups of low carb sweetener
- 1-2 teaspoons of vanilla

Combine the ingredients and whisk together in a large bowl. If the chocolate or cocoa doesn't combine well, add more as needed and include chocolate chips or shavings to enhance the flavor. Chill until the next day or for at least two hours.

Pistachio Chia Seed Pudding

Preparation time: 10 minutes (refrigerate overnight or for 2 hours)

Makes 1-2 servings

Adding a handful of crushed pistachios can add a pleasant flavor to the basic chia pudding. Pistachios can be crushed and added directly to the pudding, and/or used as a topping when serving:

- 1 cup of chia seeds
- 1 cup of coconut milk
- ½ cups cream (unsweetened) or coconut cream
- ¼ cup crushed pistachios
- ¼ cups of low carb sweetener
- 1-2 teaspoons of vanilla

Combine all ingredients, including the pistachio nuts, and reserve 1-2 tablespoons for the topping. Add more if desired. The blend will a whisk and refrigerate before serving.

Almond Chia Seed Pudding

Preparation time: 10 minutes (refrigerate overnight or for 2 hours)

Makes 1-2 servings

As an alternative to pistachio pudding, used crushed almonds and almond extract for a delicately flavored treat. Coarsely crushed almonds or meal will work well for combining directly into the ingredients. Toasted almond slices make an excellent topping just before serving:

- 1 cup of chia seeds
- 1 cup of coconut milk
- ½ cups cream (unsweetened) or coconut cream
- ¼ cups of crushed almonds
- ¼ cups of low carb sweetener
- 1-2 teaspoons of almond extract
- ¼ cups of sliced, toasted almonds (optional)

Combine all ingredients, with the exception of the sliced almonds, and whisk together. Refrigerate and prepare the almond slices just prior to serving. Lightly roast the almonds in a small skillet and set aside once they are slightly golden. Cool slightly before adding as a topping before serving.

Raspberry Chia Seed Pudding

Preparation time: 10 minutes (refrigerate overnight or for 2 hours)

Makes 1-2 servings

This recipe blends fresh raspberries with chia seeds and milk for a rich, flavorful treat:

- 1 cup of chia seeds
- 1 cup of coconut milk
- ½ cups cream (unsweetened) or coconut cream
- ¼ cups of fresh raspberries plus ½ cup for topping
- ¼ cups of low carb sweetener
- 1-2 teaspoons of almond extract

Combine all ingredients, with the exception of the ½ cup of raspberries reserved for the topping, and whisk together. Refrigerate for a minimum of two hours. Serve with the remaining fresh raspberries.

Simple Vanilla Coconut Ice Cream

Preparation time: 25 minutes (freeze for 2 hours minimum)

Makes 1-2 servings

Ice cream doesn't have to be a forbidden dessert, as it can be easily adapted to reduce or replace sugar and add only natural ingredients. Unfortunately, many store-bought ice cream brands are full of sugars, high-fructose corn syrup, and other harmful ingredients. In fact, sugar is often the least concerning the ingredients found in ice cream, as many of the additives are unnatural and provide no nutritional value. This recipe offers a simple option of combining a few ingredients for an easy, enjoyable treat:

- 1 can of coconut milk (unsweetened)
- 2 eggs
- 2 tablespoons of vanilla extract
- 2 tablespoons of low carb sweetener

Combine the coconut milk, sweetener, and vanilla extract together in a small saucepan and bring to heat, though do not bring to a boil, then reduce the heat to low or turn off completely. In a separate bowl, whisk the eggs together and slowly add and stir into the coconut milk and vanilla combination. Slowly bring the mixture back to a warm temperature, without cooking the eggs prematurely, until all four ingredients form a thick custard-like texture. Pour into an ice cream maker and refrigerate for 2-3 hours, then remove to enjoy.

Using the above recipe, a number of ingredients can be added to change and enhance the flavor:

- Add mint extract instead of vanilla, then once the mixture cools, add chocolate chips and gently fold into the ingredients, before placing in the freezer.
- Add coconut flakes to enhance this flavor.
- Stir in frozen or fresh berries before freezing.
- Add two teaspoons of ground cinnamon and ¼ cup of stewed apples for an apple-cinnamon flavor.
- Add ½ cup of pumpkin puree and two tablespoons of pumpkin spice.
- Add ½ cup of melted chocolate and 2 tablespoons of cocoa powder for a rich chocolate ice cream experience.

Peanut Butter and Banana Ice Cream

Preparation time: 25 minutes (freeze for 2 hours minimum)

Makes 1-2 servings

This is a fun and easy ice cream recipe that is completely plant-based and suitable for any diet.

- 3 ripe bananas
- 3 tablespoons of natural peanut butter (no salt or sugar added)
- 1 teaspoon of vanilla extract
- 1 pinch of cinnamon
- Dash of sea salt (optional)
- Crushed peanuts for a topping

Peel and cut all three bananas into small pieces and freeze for a couple of hours. Remove from the freezer and add to a blender or food processor, and blend with 2-3 ice cubes. Add the peanut butter, vanilla extract, sea salt, and cinnamon, then continue to blend. Remove from the blender and serve immediately. Top with the crushed peanuts.

Chocolate Hazelnut and Banana Ice Cream

Preparation time: 25 minutes (freeze for 2 hours minimum)

Makes 1-2 servings

This variation of the above recipe substitutes the chocolate and hazelnut butter for the peanut butter.

- 3 ripe bananas
- 3 tablespoons of natural hazelnut butter
- 1/8 cups of melted baker's chocolate
- 1 teaspoon of vanilla extract
- 3 teaspoons of cocoa powder
- Dash of sea salt (optional)
- Crushed hazelnuts for a topping

Peel and cut the bananas and freeze like the previous recipe. After two hours, remove from the freezer and blend with ice until smooth. Add the melted baker's chocolate, cocoa powder, and hazelnut butter and continue to blend. Add vanilla extract and the dash of sea salt, blending slightly more until smooth, then serve immediately and top with hazelnuts.

Chapter 9: Conclusion and FAQ's

Tips and Suggestions

Changing your lifestyle to include a healthier way of eating is not easy, though it can be done. For many people, the prospect of going on a diet is a temporary fix that they expect will result in a long-term result, which is never the case. In order to stick with a healthy diet, it's important to maintain focus, keep a positive outlook, and join support groups, whether it's online or in-person, or both. If you find yourself getting discouraged, just remember that this momentary and staying on track for the sake of improving your health is most important.

Here are a few tips and suggestions to keep in mind while making important changes to your diet and lifestyle:

- Try new foods and don't be afraid to taste something that's different, unique, or even unusual. Many exotic fruits and vegetables offer distinctive tastes, as well as health benefits that we may not be aware of. Mangos, guava, jackfruit, and seaweed are among some common and delicious options to try. Even some everyday foods that we pass by in the grocery store, such as avocado, aloe, lentils, and other foods that are nutritious and useful can be easily added to our everyday routine.

- Try a new recipe at least once a week, or if you're busy, once every two weeks. It doesn't have to be a complex option to impress guests, but merely a simple 3-4 ingredient dish that you enjoy. It will expand your palette and taste for new meals.
- Stay active and exercise often. Eating well is just one way to combat inflammation. Moving regularly and getting into a routine of exercise is beneficial. Studies indicate a positive impact on weight loss and health improvement from minimal exercise for 30 minutes each session for just three times a week. Walking regularly, cycling, and trying a variety of stretching and strength training exercises can help you develop muscle and tone while improving your health with diet.
- If you suffer from chronic conditions that trigger inflammation, do as much as possible to read and educate yourself on the symptoms, treatments, and what you can do to reduce the effects. Some

conditions are difficult to cure, though many of the negative side effects and pain can be greatly reduced by improving diet, exercise, and everyday habits.

- If you smoke or drink excessive alcohol, it's in your best interest to quit both, or at least reduce your drinking significantly while reducing smoking. Since both habits can be difficult to tackle, there are resources available online to curb your cravings, and eating well is one way to improve your body's condition in the meantime.

If you feel discouraged after a while and experience an increase in symptoms associated with inflammation, it's best to check in with your doctor or a specialist to monitor your health and any related condition(s). Continue to eat healthily, and if you "cheat" now and again, just start again. Everyone makes mistakes and changing dietary habits can be challenging for anyone. Sometimes, there are experiences or circumstances in life that cause us to abandon our dietary plans, and this can make returning to this diet, as with any other way of eating, challenging. Always look forward and consider the benefits of following the diet previously, which can be inspiring to begin again.

- The anti-inflammatory diet is not temporary, and it can be stopped and started at any time. Restarting is not a sign of failure and can be a new opportunity to learn about new methods, foods, and recipes to try.
- Following a set meal plan is a good start, though experimenting with new food and recipe combinations is an excellent way to become more comfortable with anti-inflammatory foods. Salads and skillet meals are great opportunities to explore a wide range of foods because both can be adapted to try any combination of vegetables and fruits. For example, adding sliced pineapples into a skillet meal with chicken is one option, while adding guava fruit in a smoothie or topping a salad is another idea that may work with certain dishes.
- Consider your diet as a food adventure, as well as a way to improve your health. It's easy to view eating plans as challenges instead of opportunities to eat differently and improve the way we live.

Frequently Asked Questions

Question: I've made significant improvements to my diet to reduce inflammation. Are there any side effects that may occur?

Answer: Unless you have any allergies or other medical conditions that may be affected by your change in diet, you should feel much better! Most people may feel the effects of cravings once you begin to abandon unhealthy foods to consume healthier options. This will eventually pass, and you'll notice that eating whole, natural foods will give you a new, positive outlook on how to take control of your health and well-being.

Question: If I have difficulty exercising due to a medical condition, will changing my diet help?

Answer: Yes, eating well and reducing inflammation, as well as other symptoms of the disease, can improve your physical condition to the point of starting an exercise routine. As with anything that can affect your health, always check with a physician first if there are risks involved. Start with simple, slow movements and limit your times, so that you become accustomed to exercise.

This is especially important if you haven't exercised in a while, as your body will need to adapt over time. Risking injury by going too quickly isn't a risk worth taking. If in doubt of your progress, consider joining a yoga or Pilates class, or consult with a personal trainer, even if for a few sessions, to get yourself started on the right path.

Question: How can I avoid buying foods that are unhealthy, while sticking to a budget?

Answer: Budgeting for groceries is often a challenge for most people, and adapting to a new diet or way of eating can increase this as well. If you are familiar with your local grocery stores, natural food stores, and farmers' markets, they are all good places to start. You may already read weekly flyers for specials and sales on specific items. Make sure you are choosing healthy food options, as often, there are sales on packaged and processed foods, which can be tempting with a limited budget. Other suggestions to get the most out of healthy eating and shopping:

- Buy from local farmers, either directly from the farm or at a local supplier. They often provide a better price than many grocery stores

- If there is a bulk store or section in your local stores, become familiar with its contents. Often, there are many dried fruits, nuts, seeds, and other ingredients that come in handy.
- Buy large amounts of specific items that you plan to use often. For example, if you use olive oil frequently, purchase a large bottle, and save money.
- Freeze any portions of foods your create that you might not finish within the week. This will prevent unnecessary waste and create a meal later when it's needed!
- Buy frozen fruits and vegetables if you don't plan to use them right away. Keep only enough fresh foods available that you plan to consume or use within the next week. Food waste is common and can be easily avoided by planning ahead.

Question: Is drinking alcohol acceptable on an anti-inflammatory diet, or should it be avoided?

Answer: Alcohol should be avoided mostly, though there are some dry wines and spirits that can be enjoyed on occasion. As a rule, it's best to avoid consuming alcohol, as it can trigger inflammation. An occasional glass of dry red or white is acceptable because there are relatively low amounts of sugar in dry wines. Liqueurs and mixed drinks or cocktails should be skipped altogether.

Question: I ate something that caused an inflammation flare-up. How can this be fixed?

Answer: It's perfectly normal to eat something that can cause inflammation, either because we're not familiar with specific food and its effects on our body. For this reason, it's best to find relief by resting until the condition is improved. Take note of any and all foods that cause inflammation and other unpleasant effects on your body.

Question: Should I go vegan to improve my chances of reducing and/or eliminating inflammation altogether?

Answer: Going vegan is definitely an excellent option, though it isn't necessary in order to fight inflammation and reap the benefits of an anti-inflammation diet. By eliminating processed foods, refined, and unnatural foods, you'll increase your health significantly. While it is advisable to remove as much red meat from your diet as possible, lean cuts of beef are acceptable in moderation and in combination with other non-inflammatory foods.

Question: Are organic foods a better option? Is there a reason to choose locally grown and harvested foods as opposed to imported?

Answer: Depending on where you live, you may have some foods locally available, which is beneficial and advantageous. Local, organic foods tend to be fresher and contain fewer pesticides, and may also cost less. Some imported foods are excellent for an anti-inflammatory diet and should be included as well. Make an effort to eat and promote as many local foods as possible, while selecting the best, highest quality imported fruits and vegetables. Meats are best to purchase from a local butcher or farmers' market to ensure freshness and high quality.

Question: Are there any plant-based foods that should be avoided that may trigger inflammation?

Answer: Fortunately, all fruits and vegetables are excellent for the anti-inflammation diet. Unless you suffer from an allergic reaction or simply choose not to eat specific fruits or vegetables, any variety can be chosen and enjoyed with your meal. For best results and maximum enjoyment of this diet, try new foods that you've never had before to get a sense of what options are available to you. When most people change their way of eating, even for the better, they often focus on the restrictions, instead of the benefits of changing their habits. There are a lot of opportunities in the world of fresh fruits, vegetables, nuts, and seeds, among other non-inflammatory foods. Getting familiar with new local foods or exotic fruits, for example, can be fun and inspire you to attempt new recipes.

Question: Should all dairy products be avoided, or can certain milk products remain in an anti-inflammatory diet?

Answer: Most dairy products can contribute to inflammation, though they don't have to be entirely removed from your diet. It's best to stick with dairy items that are less likely to trigger inflammation, such as goat cheese, yogurt, and skim milk. Other dairy products can be used in moderation, as long as the majority of your food, ideally, 90 percent, is anti-inflammatory. If you find that limiting dairy isn't enough, you may want to consider using soy or other vegan-based yogurts and milk.

Question: Where can I find vegan-based dairy products? I'm new to plant-based foods and would like to try some.

Answer: Long gone are the days when vegan diets were considered a fad or unique way of eating. It wasn't that long ago when searching for anything plant-based was hard to find and required visiting a natural food store. Currently, every grocery store has a plant-based, vegan-friendly section, often located close to or within the produce section. This makes finding a wide variety of vegan meats, cheeses, tofu, tempeh, and miso-based foods easy and effortless. Non-dairy milk is often featured alongside dairy products, as well as often vegan cheese and yogurt products. Many of the products are soy, vegetable, or coconut-milk based.

Question: Are there any varieties of fish that should be avoided on an anti-inflammation diet?

Answer: Overall, fish is safe and healthy. Unless you have allergies to fish or fish products, or concerns about the quality of seafood in your region, it remains a healthy part of many diets and promotes anti-inflammatory properties. If you have concerns about the quality of seafood, or product recalls, monitor the news and contact your local businesses with questions. Some types of fish, such as tuna, raise issues about mercury contamination, and there are some worries about the safety of farm fishing. If in doubt, research your fish options and avoid any varieties that seem questionable. It's always best to take precautions than risks.

Question: Is pork allowed with an anti-inflammatory diet?

Answer: Pork is not recommended as an anti-inflammatory food, though it can be enjoyed in small portions and in moderation. Beef and chicken are good alternatives and can often take the place of pork in most meals and recipes. Bacon is available as chicken and turkey varieties, and also as a vegan "bacon." While no foods are strictly forbidden on the anti-inflammatory diet, pork should be avoided mostly because it can have negative effects on the body. An occasional indulgence is always an option!

Question: How easy is it to follow the anti-inflammation diet while on vacation or where there are fewer different food options available?

Answer: This would depend on where you choose to travel and what foods are available. If you take a vacation in a tropical or warm climate, there are often many fresh fruits and vegetables to choose from, and generally, there are no issues with finding foods to support the way you eat. In northern climates, where meat and fish are more common than fresh produce, there may be less to choose from, though fish is always a good idea. You may want to avoid bread and other processed or refined foods, though, in moderation, they can be acceptable and may not cause any reactions.

There is a challenge where there are no fresh foods or meats available and most of the choices are processed. While this is unlikely, it's always good to research ahead to know exactly which types of food options are available before you travel. For example, if you are traveling to a remote location, confirm there are enough options available to suit your dietary needs. This can be a challenge for people who follow a plant-based diet, though now more than ever, many restaurants are accommodating and often offer vegan options.

Questions: My doctor advised me against eating vegan, though I prefer a plant-based diet because it works best to prevent inflammation. Is there anything I can do?

Answer: Most health professionals are aware of the benefits of vegan diets, though not everyone agrees they are the best option. If you are confident that a plant-based diet is still best for you, ask your doctor which specific nutrients you need more of, which will enable you to research options for plant-based options, such as:

- B12 is most commonly available in red meat, though it can be found in miso and brewer's yeast
- Vitamin D is found in many non-dairy kinds of milk and products, as well as their dairy counterparts.

- Dark green vegetables, lentils, and many nuts and seeds, among many other plant-based foods, are adequately high in calcium, protein, and minerals.

There may be specific health concerns a doctor or specialist has that cannot be addressed on an individual basis, though for most people, plant-based eating is considered safe and healthy, with no adverse effects.

Question: Is inflammation attributed to the way we eat in the first place?

Answer: The cause of inflammation varies from being the body's way of fighting off disease and infection to a sign of a chronic health condition. This can become to detect if you experience inflammation without any known medical conditions that contribute to it. If you spent many years eating inflammation-producing foods, this can be part of the reason for its cause, which makes a change in diet even more vital. Most people know the source of inflammation, either because they've been diagnosed with a specific disorder or disease or know which food(s) triggers it. Knowing the cause can definitely help with treatment, though having a good meal plan is more of a preventative approach.

The way most people eat is based on convenience first, followed by taste and health. When you realize that the way you eat is causing your health and body to feel worse, those priorities will change, even temporarily, until the negative symptoms subside. Priority should still focus on taste and experience with foods, though health should become the most important factor in how we choose the meals we eat. Once this is done, we can move away from treatment and towards prevention.

Question: Is there a risk of irregularity or other changes in bodily functions from starting an anti-inflammation diet?

Answer: There are only positive results! Changes in the way your body digests and processes food will only improve, and this will have a good impact on your metabolism. There should be no issues with irregularity, and if anything changes, it will be in a positive direction. Sometimes, our body may react a certain way if we're not used to eating certain foods, and any sensations we might experience will likely be temporary.

Questions: Is there an age range where the benefits of the anti-inflammation diet work best?

Answer: This diet can work at any age! It's a healthy way to eat for anyone, whether you experience chronic conditions or not, or whether inflammation is an issue because the diet is balanced, healthy, and focuses on natural, whole foods as opposed to processed and refined options. Eating a diet rich in whole foods is one of the best ways to prevent many forms of the disease, and beginning at a young age is safe and healthy, provided you are not deficient in any nutrients and eat regular meals.

For older adults, this diet can be life-changing, as there are often more medical concerns as we advance in age. Keeping active and eating well are two of the most important ways to age well and remain healthy for many years.

Question: How can I keep on top of my diet and make sure I'm getting the most out of the anti-inflammation diet?

Answer: Everyone will benefit from this diet, whether inflammation is a recurring issue or not. To maximize the benefits of this way of eating, research as much as possible, searching for apps and tools online for advice and tracking your food choices. A simple grocery list app can be a lot of help in organizing and budgeting for the foods you buy and eat on a regular basis. There are apps that track the number of carbs you consume (for the ketogenic diet) as well as calorie-counters. Joining a social media group dedicated to supporting and learning from others about the benefits of anti-inflammatory foods is a great opportunity to understand and relate to others who may face the same or similar challenges in life.

Question: Can I combine this diet with other ways of eating, such as low carb, ketogenic, and/or intermittent fasting?

Answer: If you have no major health conditions that could be impacted by another way of eating, then it's likely that both can be combined to benefit you of health. To be certain, always check with a health professional first to ensure you're able to combine another way of eating into your lifestyle. For example, some people with type 2 diabetes experience significant improvement with the keto diet, which includes a lot of food options available in the anti-inflammation diet. On the other hand, the intermittent fasting diet may not be recommended for people with irregular blood sugar and glucose levels, while the anti-inflammation diet works for them and improves their health. Every individual has specific needs that can be met with some diets more than others.

Question: If I'm athletic and generally active, will my body be able to handle processed foods better?

Answer: If you are in good health and already active, the anti-inflammation diet is a good plan for prevention, though even moderate consumption of processed foods should be avoided, especially if you exercise regularly. This is because your body needs the fuel of a higher value, and to function and perform well, improving your diet is paramount because you will likely burn everything you consume within a short period of time. If you add unhealthy foods, this will create a temporary deficit in nutrients, and you may notice a fluctuation in energy levels. For this reason, avoid any high sugar and/or high salt foods, though if you choose to enjoy them, drink plenty of water and choose something healthier.

Question: Should I avoid fast food?

Answer: Traditionally, fast foods are deep-fried and contain a lot of additives that should be avoided. Fortunately, there are many alternatives available, such as salads, soups, and low carb options that cater to more dietary options, including plant-based diets. There are many food outlets that offer freshly squeezed juices and smoothies, which can be a good option, though beware of added sugars in so-called "healthy" smoothies. Visit salad bars and try drinking your coffee or tea sugar-free. There are many little changes that can make a big difference. There are always healthier options to replace the unhealthy foods and drinks we see every day, and all it takes is a bit of willpower and a drive to improve how we eat to succeed.

Made in the USA
Columbia, SC
10 September 2020